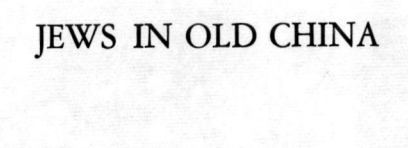

JEWS IN OLD CHINA

# JEWS IN OLD CHINA

Some Western Views

Compiled and with an Introduction
by
HYMAN KUBLIN

PARAGON BOOK REPRINT CORP.
NEW YORK
1971

Copyright© 1971 by Paragon Book Reprint Corp.

Library of Congress Catalog Card No.: 70-152838

Manufactured in the United States of America
by Arno Press, New York

To

## DR. RUDOLPH LOEWENTHAL

Yet fearing that after a lapse of time this story would not be handed on, he desired to have it cut on stone to be transmitted to future generations....

from: *K'aifeng Monumental Inscription, 1663*

## Table of Contents

I. Preface .............................. ix
II. Introduction ........................ xi
III. *The Jews in China: Their Synagogue, Their Scriptures, Their History,* by James Finn ... 1
IV. *Chinese Jews; a Lecture* by Marcus N. Adler. 93
V. *The History of the Jews in China* by S. M. Perlmann. ................... 119
VI. *Chinese Jews* by Edward I. Ezra and Arthur Sopher ...................... 213

*Preface*

*Jews in Old China* is the second of several volumes composed of materials written about the Jewish inhabitants of the old Chinese Empire republished by the Paragon Book Reprint Corp. of New York City. These materials, comprising books, brochures, and scholarly studies, have for years been out of print and in perennial demand by scholars and students concerned with the fields of the history of the Jews in China and Chinese studies. It is hoped that their easier availability in the form of these reprints will facilitate scholarship and also help satisfy the intellectual curiosity of interested laymen in both East and West. *Jews in Old China* was preceded by *Studies of the Chinese Jews; Selected Articles from Journals East and West*. The third volume scheduled for publication in this series is a reprint of *The Orphan Colony of Jews in China* by James Finn, which originally appeared in London in 1872.

For assistance in the preparation of this volume the generous cooperation of several institutions and many individuals is gratefully acknowledged. Particular mention must be made of the following: the Library of the Jewish Theological Seminary of America; the YIVO Institute for Jewish Research of New York City; Dr. Rudolph Loewenthal; Prof. David Kranzler; Mr. Arthur Sopher; and Mr. Samuel Sokobin.

*Hyman Kublin*

## Introduction

About 1605, so the standard account has it, an unusual visitor made his way to the home of Father Matteo Ricci in Peking. The Jesuit missionary, who had lived and worked in the Chinese Empire for almost a quarter of a century, was doubtless better informed on things Chinese than any European of his times. But he was frankly at a loss to identify his visitor. "His whole external appearance, nose, eyes, and all his facial lineaments," it is reported, "were anything but Chinese."[1] But, as conversation progressed, it began to dawn upon Ricci "that he was talking with a believer in the ancient Jewish law."[2] Soon learning that communities of Jews existed in scattered areas of China, the Jesuit missionary suddenly realized how limited had been his awareness of the geographical dimensions of the Jewish Diaspora.[3]

News of Ricci's "discovery" of the Chinese Jews was in due time transmitted to the Papacy in Rome. Ultimately his reports and supplementary information became known to European officials and traders in the East and to scholars and clerics in the West.[4] Still, their hope for further data about Jews in the Chinese Empire was never to be completely satisfied. For more than a century after Ricci's day the Jesuits had little incentive to search out the answers to questions that titillated the imagination of Westerners. Being gravely undermanned in their proselytizing enterprises and having other concerns competing for their attention, they pursued their inquiries only infrequently. As a result, European knowledge of the Chinese Jews was for many years based mainly upon the occasional reports written and materials collected by the Jesuits in the seventeenth and early eighteenth centuries.[5]

Despite the paucity of solid and reliable information, discussions and speculations about the Chinese Jews cropped up from time to time in the writings of Europeans for several hundred years.[6] Almost all these notices were essentially derivative, ranging from the sober and reflective to the utterly fanciful. While the vast part of this literature is of interest primarily to bibliographers and historiographers, several of these pioneering studies are still worthy of our attention. Among eighteenth-century scholars mention must be made of the contributions of the Jesuit Father Ignaz Kögler and of the French savant, Silvrestre de Sacy; in the early nineteenth century the studies of the German theologian, Christian von Murr, are preeminent.[7] This early chapter in the history of and about the Chinese Jews was closed in 1843 with the publication of a remarkable little book by James Finn, an English scholar and diplomat.

Anyone who ploughs through the literature on the Jews in the Chinese Empire before mid-nineteenth century can only be impressed by Finn's *The Jews in China*. It is not simply that the Englishman combed patiently and methodically through all the available literature on the subject. He also possessed what many earlier writers had not enjoyed, namely, a fine grasp of Jewish history and Judaism. Careful in the evaluation of his sources, he was circumspect in the formulation of his conclusions.

It is therefore not surprising that for many years, even in our own times, students of the history of the Chinese Jews have leaned heavily upon Finn's book.

James Finn, born in England in 1806, became deeply interested as a young man in the purposes and activities of the London Society for Promoting Christianity among the Jews. Studying Hebrew by himself, his researches into the history of the Jews in the Diaspora led him to the library collections in the British Museum. Here he discovered the *Lettres Edifiantes et Curieuses* of the Jesuits, in which were included the reports from the missionaries in China. The literature so intrigued him that he read everything he could find on the subject. The fruit of his studies was *The Jews in China*.

The publication of Finn's monograph was most timely. It appeared in the year following the conclusion of the momentous Treaty of Nanking which terminated the so-called Opium War between Great Britain and China. According to its provisions, five ports along the China Coast were opened to the residence and trade of Westerners, while the island of Hong Kong was ceded to Great Britain.[8] In the years immediately after the Treaty small communities of foreigners, notably merchants and missionaries, were established in the "treaty ports." Some of them were eager to learn as much as they could about the Middle Kingdom and the results of their studies were widely read both locally and in the West. A local publication, the *Chinese Repository*, had become standard reading fare for "treaty port" residents. Long extracts from Finn's book were reprinted in the periodical, with the result that pioneer "China hands" were alerted to the presence of Jews in the Chinese Empire.[9]

In the fall of 1845 Finn was appointed to the post of His Majesty's Consul in Jerusalem. He assumed his formal duties in the following year and remained in Palestine until 1862. Because of failing health Finn returned to England where he spent the remaining years of his life. To the end of his days he continued to collect information about the Chinese Jews. He died in 1872, in the same year that his work, *The Orphan Colony of Jews in China*, was published.[10]

Finn had hoped that with the opening of the treaty ports in China opportunities would be offered to establish contact with Jews in the interior of the country, especially with the community at K'aifeng.[11] There had been no word from or about this Jewish group since it was visited by Jesuit missionaries more than a hundred years before. In 1844 Finn composed a Hebrew letter to the K'aifeng Jews and arranged for its delivery. Patient though he was, many years passed before he received a reply.[12] Nevertheless, he was delighted to learn that in the winter of 1850-1851 two Chinese converts to Christianity, despatched by Bishop George Smith of Victoria, Hong Kong, succeeded in reaching the city and finding members of the old Jewish community.[13] This mission was truly a landmark in the history of the Chinese Jews. Unfortunately events within China deterred further contacts for a number of years.

The spread of the T'aiping Rebellion (1849-1864) disrupted travel and communications in large parts of the Chinese Empire. Not even the arrangements provided for in the new treaties concluded by the Western powers with China in 1858 and 1860, permitting travel into the interior of the Chinese Empire, could induce many Westerners to stray far from their treaty port sanctuaries. But in 1866, when a semblance of internal peace and order was restored, the American Protestant missionary, W. L. P. Martin, made his way to K'aifeng; his reports were widely read around the world. Another valuable report was prepared by J. L. Liebermann, an Austrian Jewish trader, who visited the city in 1867.[14] During the remaining years of the nineteenth century, accounts of the K'aifeng Jewish community, usually based upon earlier reports, continued to appear in European and Western journals.

What Finn had done for earlier generations in recapitulating knowledge of the Chinese Jews was redone by Marcus Nathan Adler at the turn of the twentieth century. He was born in Hannover, Germany, in 1837, into a renowned rabbinical family. The Adlers emigrated to England and in 1844 Marcus's father (Nathan Marcus) was appointed Chief Rabbi; in effect, he was Chief Rabbi of the British Empire. As for Marcus himself, he was educated at University College in London and thereafter pursued a business career as an actuary for the Alliance Assurance Company. Adler's business activities constituted only a small part of an otherwise full life. Esteemed as a mathematician, he was a fellow of the Royal Statistical Society and a founder of the London Mathematical Society. For a time he was also the confidential secretary to Sir Moses Montefiore, business tycoon and peerless champion of Jewish causes during his long life.

Like other members of his family, Adler devoted much time to study of the history of the Jewish people. Exactly when and how he became interested in the historical problems of the Chinese Jews is uncertain. Many influences, however, were at play. It may well be that the matter was brought to his attention by Montefiore who, as an old acquaintance of James Finn, must have known about his research and writing.[15] It is possible too that his curiosity was aroused by the references of the famed medieval traveler, Benjamin of Tudela, in whose classical travelogue Adler had an absorbing interest.[16] Not to be overlooked, moreover, is the stimulus provided by Adolph Neubauer's study of the Chinese Jews which appeared in the *Jewish Quarterly Review* (London), in 1895. It is pertinent that Marcus's younger brother, Elkan, wrote a long piece on Oriental Jewry in the same publication a few years later, in which he commented upon portions of Neubauer's study.[17]

Be all this as it may, Adler presented a long lecture on the subject of the Chinese Jews before the Jews' College Literary Society in London on June 17, 1900. Basically he retraced much of the same ground marked out by Finn several generations before. But by diligent research he succeeded in gathering together considerable information about the efforts of Westerners to establish relations with the K'aifeng Jewish community from mid-nineteenth century on. Adler's lecture was extensively reported upon in the London *Jewish Chronicle* on June 22. Thereafter it was published in entirety in London and was then translated into German, Hebrew, and Yiddish.[18]

Adler's study was published at a time when an unprecedented wave of interest in the Chinese Jews and their history was mounting in both China and the West. Increasingly, articles of a popular nature appeared in newspapers and magazines around the world. Most of these accounts added little or nothing to knowledge of the subject. More important, however, were the scholarly studies which were occasionally published in learned journals in East and West. Unquestionably the major work of scholarship on the Chinese Jews during this era was the translation of the inscriptions on the stone tablets which had been preserved for hundreds of years by the K'aifeng Jewish community. In many respects this work of scholarship by the Jesuit, Father Jerome Tobar, has yet to be superseded.[19]

Unusual among the studies of the history of the Chinese Jews which appeared in the early twentieth century were the writings of S. M. Perlmann. Unfortunately little is known about his personal or professional life. Internal evidence in his works indicates that he visited China a short while before he undertook to publicize the story of the Chinese Jews. His initial contribution, *The Jews in China*, was published in London in 1909, while excerpts and translations from this work appeared in Hebrew and Russian about the same time. Four years later Perlmann published a longer study, *The History of the Jews in China*, in which he embodied the results of further research and reflection.

Perlmann made little substantive contribution to knowledge about the Chinese Jews. He was evidently far more at home in the field of Jewish studies than in what was for Westerners at this period the esoteric realm of Sinology. He did, however, add a novel dimension to the common conclusions that had for years been drawn from the Jewish historical experience in the Chinese empire. In Perlmann's opinion the fate of the Chinese Jews, absorbed in the course of time by the people and civilization of China, argued strongly for the need of Jews to establish a national home for themselves. "We need not look for testimonies into the histories of other nations," he wrote,[20]

> as we ourselves have had enough experiences: we have seen that the Jews have nearly been absorbed in free countries like Italy and France, we have seen that the Jews have become totally extinct in China ... the danger is not imminent in those countries where the hostility to the Jews is still strong and effective, because they will fight there and conserve

themselves.... Therefore we have to look out for means to prevent the process of absorption, and *the only remedy is, as I have said, a territory for the Jews.*

Only four years after Perlmann enunciated his opinion Great Britain issued the Balfour Declaration, stating its support for the establishment of a "national home for the Jewish people" in Palestine.

The stream of writings about the Chinese Jews at the turn of the twentieth century sharpened the awareness of residents in the treaty ports of China of the existence of the Jewish community at K'aifeng. Members of the Jewish community of Shanghai, consisting mainly of foreigners who had settled in the city after the Sino-Japanese War (1894-1895), finally determined to take measures for the relief of their religious brethren in the interior. On May 14, 1900, the Society for the Rescue of the Chinese Jews was founded. Its declared purposes were: [21]

To study the origin, development, and history of the Jewish Colonies in China; to preserve such sites and monuments as exist, and erect monuments where advantageous; to bring back to Judaism any Chinese Jews lineally descended from Jewish families.

The Society met from time to time during the next four years.[22] Contacts were established with the K'aifeng Jews, several of whom were induced to come to Shanghai where they received religious instruction. But despite its efforts, the Society was unsuccessful in raising adequate funds for the realization of its purposes. Potential donors in Europe and America, more immediately concerned with the plight of millions of Jews in Russia and eastern Europe, were reluctant to rally to the support of the Society. In March, 1904, its activities were quietly suspended.

A key member of the Rescue Society was Edward Isaac Ezra,[23] who was born in Shanghai in 1881. He ultimately prospered by financial and real estate ventures. Shortly after he interviewed a group of K'aifeng Jews in his home in the spring of 1902 he published a long study, "Chinese Jews," in the *East of Asia Magazine*, a new periodical which had just been launched in Shanghai.[24] It contained little new information about the Chinese Jews but did throw light upon the activities of the Rescue Society. An important feature of Ezra's piece was the illustrative matter. Many of his photographs of the K'aifeng Jews and their environs were original; in later years some of them embellished the works of other writers.

After World War I had drawn to a close, efforts were made to revive the Society for the Rescue of the Chinese Jews. Some of the participants in the new campaign had been members of the earlier organization; others, such as George Sokolsky, who was to acquire worldwide fame as a writer and commentator on the revolutionary scene in China, represented a new generation of Jewish residents in China.[25] To promote interest in the work of the Rescue Society Arthur Sopher, a brother-in-law of Edward Isaac Ezra, reprinted Ezra's earlier study, to which he added a long section detailing developments concerning the Chinese Jews during the preceding two decades. Entitled *Chinese Jews*, the brochure was published in Shanghai in 1926.

For almost twenty years after the publication of Sopher's work accounts of the Chinese Jews continued to appear in magazines and journals around the world. In the 1930's, however, discussions of the Chinese Jews had to compete for attention with reports about Jewish refugees from Naziism who were then seeking temporary haven in Shanghai and other places in the East. Still, this new type of literature did not deter scholars from pursuing their studies of the Jews in the old Chinese Empire. In 1939 Dr. Rudolph Loewenthal, a German-born scholar residing in Peking, issued the first of his many bibliographies on the subject of the Chinese Jews.[26] His work has been indispensable to every scholar ever since. In 1942 another monumental work concerned with "Chinese Jewish" studies appeared, the three-volume opus of Bishop William Charles White, a Canadian missionary in China, which gathered together much but not all of the extant source materials and related scholarly and popular studies.[27] That this work went out of print within a few years after its publication was in itself testimony to the perennial interest in those Jews and their descendants who made their home in the Chinese Empire for almost a thousand years.

Brooklyn College of the
   City University of New York       *Hyman Kublin*

### Notes

1. Louis J. Gallagher, S. J. *China in the Sixteenth Century: the Journals of Matthew Ricci: 1583-1610.* translated from the Latin. (New York, Random House, 1953), p. 107.
2. *Ibid.*, p. 108.
3. Catholic missionaries and other Westerners had made their way to the Far East several centuries before, especially during the era of Mongol ascendancy. Though several of them had reported the presence of Jews in Central Asia and China, presumably this information was not known to Ricci and his colleagues. See: A. C. Moule, *Christians in China before the Year 1500* (New York, 1930), *passim.*

4. See in this respect the notes on Dom Luis de Menezes, a Portuguese official in India, in: Charles R. Boxer, *Fidalgos in the Far East, 1550-1770,* (The Hague, Martinus Nijhoff, 1948), p.213.

5. A useful inventory of this data will be found in: Donald D. Leslie, "The Kaifeng Jewish Community: a Summary," *Jewish Journal of Sociology,* XI, no.2 (December, 1969), p.184. This entire article is reprinted in Hyman Kublin (comp.), *Studies of the Chinese Jews* (New York, Paragon Book Reprint Corp.), 1970.

6. An informative survey of such references appears in Rudolph Loewenthal, "Jews in China in Eighteenth Century Literature," *Historia Judaica,* XII (1950), pp. 67-74.

7. For particulars of their publications see: Rudolph Loewenthal, "The Jews in China; an Annotated Bibliography," *Chinese Social and Political Science Review,* XXIV (1940), pp. 167; 141; and 189.

8. Reversing policies which had prevailed during earlier years of their dynasty, the Manchu rulers of China had by 1760 restricted the maritime trade of Westerners to the sole port of Canton.

9. The *Chinese Repository* (20 volumes) was published from May, 1832, to December, 1851. It was reprinted in Tokyo in the 1960's. The extracts from Finn's book appear in volume XIV, no. 7 (July, 1845), pp. 305-334 and no. 8 (August, 1845), pp. 388-395.

10. This book is scheduled for republication by the Paragon Book Reprint Corp. in 1971.

11. For the K'aifeng Jewish community, see especially Leslie, *loc. cit.*, pp. 176 ff.

12. For particulars as well as the text of Finn's letter see: James Finn, *The Orphan Colony of Jews in China* (London, 1872), pp. 12 ff.

13. The report of this enterprise is presented in George Smith and W. H. Medhurst, *A Narrative of a Mission of Inquiry to the Jewish Synagogue of K'aifung-fu on Behalf of the London Society for Promoting Christianity among the Jews,* (Shanghai, 1851).

14. See, *inter alia,* W. L. P. Martin, *A Cycle of Cathay,* 2nd ed., New York, 1897, pp. 265-279. Liebermann's account, translated and edited by A. Löwy, will be found in the *Report of the Anglo-Jewish Association for 1879* (London), pp. 90-96 (Appendix E). It is entitled "Notes on the Jews in China."

15. Elizabeth Anne MacCaul, *Reminiscences of Mrs. Finn* (London, 1930), pp. 84-85; 137 ff.
16. Adler ultimately published a translation from the Hebrew of the travels of Benjamin of Tudela: *The Itinerary of Benjamin of Tudela* (Oxford, 1907).
17. Neubauer's study is reprinted in Hyman Kublin, cited above. Elkan Adler's references to the Chinese Jews will be found in his study, "The Persian Jews: Their Books and Their Ritual," *Jewish Quarterly Review* (London), X (1898), especially pp. 601-602 and 624-625.
18. The particulars of these translations are presented in Loewenthal's bibliography, cited above, p. 136.
19. Jerome Tobar, S. J., *Inscriptions juives de K'ai-fong-fou*. 1st ed. (Shanghai, 1900), 2nd ed. (Shanghai, 1912).
20. S. M. Perlmann, *The History of the Jews in China*, (London, 1913), pp. 93-94.
21. Edward Isaac Ezra and Arthur Sopher, *Chinese Jews* (Shanghai, 1926), p. 76.
22. A sketch of the Society's activities appears in William Charles White, *Chinese Jews*, 3 vols., Toronto, 1942, I, 152 ff. See also the 2nd edition, three volumes in one, published in 1966.
23. Not related to Nissim Ezra Benjamin Ezra who founded the newspaper *Israel's Messenger* in Shanghai in 1904.
24. Edward Isaac Ezra, "Chinese Jews," *East of Asia Magazine*, I, (1902), pp. 278-296.
25. See Sokolsky's article "The Jews in China," *Menorah Journal*, XV, no. 5 (November, 1928), pp. 453-456.
26. Loewenthal's bibliography, "The Jews in China: a Bibliography," first appeared in *Yenching Journal of Social Studies*, I, no. 2 (January, 1939), pp. 256-291. Considerably expanded, it was then published in the *Chinese Social and Political Science Review*, XXIV (1940), pp. 118-261. Note should also be taken of Loewenthal's "The Early Jews in China: a Supplementary Bibliography," *Folklore Studies* (Peiping), V (1946), pp. 353-398.
27. See note 22.

# THE JEWS

IN

# CHINA:

THEIR SYNAGOGUE, THEIR SCRIPTURES,

THEIR HISTORY, &c.

BY JAMES FINN,

AUTHOR OF "SEPHARDIM;" OR, HISTORY OF THE JEWS IN SPAIN AND PORTUGAL.

---

" They built a synagogue, and in it laid up sacred books which concern not only themselves but all men; kings and subjects, parents and children, the old and the young."—INSCRIPTION AT KAE-FUNG-FOO.

---

刀筋教

# PREFACE.

This little work may serve to call attention to a very peculiar branch of the children of Israel, to whom but an occasional allusion, almost without remark, has hitherto been made in this country.

Rather more has been done on the Continent, and some learned foreigners have written disquisitions upon various points of the subject; yet all have been too much contented to give the bare statements of the missionaries, with their mistakes and inconsequences; not always citing even these with precision, and therefore differing somewhat from each other. The present digest is by no means a mere translation.

For the sake of a uniform orthography in European letters, the Chinese names and terms here cited are regulated by Dr. Morrison's Dictionary, and his "View of China for Philological Purposes," the vowels having their

## PREFACE.

English sound.  The difference of spelling the same words in the various books referred to, is often sufficiently amusing.

We are indebted for our present knowledge of the Chinese Jews to the Jesuit missionaries in that country. Let us hope to receive new information concerning them from future missionaries, who shall preach only according to the written word of God, who shall be free from the least taint of idolatry; men animated with zeal for the salvation of mankind, and at the same time rendering obedience to ecclesiastical discipline.

The new position of England, arising from the Treaty of Nan-king, 29th August, 1842, ought to encourage many such men to proclaim Christianity in that Empire. Facilities of various kinds for such a work are now before us. The Jews there will be unimpeachable witnesses to the truth of the Old Testament,— the New Testament and our scriptural Liturgy are already rendered into Chinese by English predecessors in the field,—and we may rest assured that the Divine blessing will not be wanting to sanction every effort made in promoting the spiritual good of China.

## LIST OF BOOKS
### REFERRING TO THE JEWS IN CHINA.

---

1. Trigaltius, de Christianâ Expeditione apud Sinas. Aug. Vind. 1615, p. 118.
2. Imperio de la China, i cultura evangelica en él. Por el P. Alvaro Semmedo. Madrid, 1642, p. 196.
3. Lettres édifiantes et curieuses, Recueil vii. Paris, 1707. Lettre 1re.
4. Duhalde, Description de la Chine. Fol., Paris, 1735, tom. iii. p. 64.
5. Deguignes, Histoire générale des Huns, &c. Paris, 1756, p. 26.
6. Brotier, Tacitus, Paris, 1771, tom. iii. p. 567. The dissertation on this subject is omitted in the later editions.
7. Kennicott, Dissertatio generalis in Biblia Hebraica. Fol., Oxon., 1776, p. 65.
8. Michaelis, Orientalische Bibliothek. Th. v. p. 70; Th. ix. p. 40; Th. xv. p. 15.
9. Lettres édifiantes et curieuses, Recueil xxxi.
10. Eichhorn, Einleitung in das alte Testament. Leipzig, 1781. Th. ii. p. 131.
11. Murr (Chr. Theoph. de) Diarii litterarii. Halæ, 1797. Th. ix. p. 81.

12. Murr (Chr. Gottlieb von) Neues Journal zur litteratur und kunstgeschichte. Leipzig, 1798. Th. i. p. 147.

13. Cibot (Pierre) Digression sur le temps ou les Juifs ont passé in Chine, dans les "Memoires concernant l'histoire, les mœurs, &c., des Chinois." Par les Missionnaires de Pekin. Paris, 1791, tom. xv. p. 52.

14. Kæglerii (P. Ignatii.) Notitiæ S.S. Bibliorum Judæorum in Imperio Sinensi. Halæ, 1805. This is a reprint from the "Neues Journal," &c., of Murr., Th. vii., and accompanied by the treatises, 1. De Sacy de ærâ Judæorum Sinensium. 2. Chr. Theoph. de Murr., "Series chronologica rerum Judaicarum in imperio Sinensi." 3. Cibot, reprinted from the above-mentioned "Memoires concernant," &c.

15. Traité de la Chronologie Chinoise par le P. Gaubil, et publié par De Sacy. Paris, 1814, p. 264.

16. Jewish Expositor. London, 1816, pp. 101, 135, 414.

17. Grosier, Description de la Chine. Paris, 1819, tom. iv. p. 484.

18. Calmet's Dictionary of the Bible. London, 1823. Vol. iv., p. 251.

19. Sionnet (L'Abbé) Essai sur les Juifs de la Chine. Paris, 1837.

# THE JEWS IN CHINA.

## CHAPTER I.

### DISCOVERY AND INTERCOURSE.

The Jesuit missionaries were but a short time settled in Pe-king, when one summer's day, at the beginning of the seventeenth century, a visitor called upon Father Matthew Ricci, induced to do so by an account then recently published in the metropolis, of the foreigners who worshipped a single Lord of heaven and earth, and yet were not Mohammedans. Entering the house with a smile, he announced himself as one of the same religion with its inmates. The missionary remarking how much his features and figure differed from those prevailing among the Chinese, led him to the chapel. It was St. John Baptist's-day, and over the altar was a painting of the Virgin Mary with the

Infant Jesus, and the future Baptist on his knees before them. The stranger bowed to the picture as Ricci did, but explained at the same time, that he was not accustomed to do so before any such representations; only he could not refrain from paying the usual homage of the country to his great ancestors. Beside the altar were pictures of the four evangelists. He inquired if these were not of the twelve? Ricci answered in the affirmative, supposing him to mean the twelve apostles. Then, returning to the first apartment, he proposed questions in turn, and an unexpected explanation ensued. The stranger was a descendant of Israel, and during his survey of the chapel, had imagined the large picture to represent Rebekah with Jacob and Esau, and the other persons to denote four of the sons of Jacob.

It was some time before this simple explanation could be elicited, on account of the misunderstanding on both sides, which impeded the use of direct interrogation. The visitor, however, knew nothing of the appellation, Jew: he styled himself an Israelite, by name Ngai, a native of Kae-fung-foo, the capital of the province, Ho-nan, where, having prepared himself by study for a Mandarin degree, he had now repaired to Pe-king for his examination; and, led by curiosity or a fellow-feeling for the supposed fraternity of his nation, he had thus ventured to call at the mission-house.

He stated, that in his native city there were ten or twelve families of Israelites, with a fair synagogue, which they had recently restored and decorated at an expense of ten thousand crowns,[1] and in which they preserved a roll of the law, four or five hundred years old; adding, that in Hang-chow-foo, the capital of Che-keang, there were considerably more families, with their synagogue.

He made several allusions to events and persons of Scripture history, but pronounced the names differently from the mode usual in Europe. When shown a Hebrew Bible he was unable to read it, though he at once recognised the characters. He said, that Hebrew learning was still maintained among his people, that his brother was proficient in it; and he seemed to confess that his own neglect of it, with preference for Gentile literature, had exposed him to censure from the congregation and the rabbi;[2]

[1] Decem aureorum millibus instaurârant.—*Trigaut.*
[2] None of the missionaries use this word; but in Latin they say, "Archisynagogus," and in French, "Chef de

but this gave him little concern, as his ambition aimed at the honours to be gained from Chinese learning—a disciple rather of Confucius than of Moses.

Three years afterwards, having had no earlier opportunity, Ricci despatched a Chinese Christian to investigate, at Kae-fung-foo, the truth of this singular discovery. All was found to be as described, and the messenger brought back with him a copy of the titles and endings of the five books of Moses. These were compared with the printed Plantinian Bible, and found to correspond exactly: the writing, however, had no vowel-points. Ricci, ignorant of Hebrew, commissioned the same native convert to return with an epistle, in Chinese, addressed to the rabbi, announcing that at Pe-king he was possessor of all the other books of the Old Testament, as well as those of the New Testament, which contains a record of the acts of Messiah, who is already come. In reply, the rabbi asserted that Messiah is not only not come, but that he would not appear for ten thousand years. He added, that having heard of the fame of his correspondent, he would

la synagogue;" but we shall find reason to justify the use of the more familiar term.

willingly transfer to him the government of the synagogue, if Ricci would abstain from swine's flesh, and reside with the community.

Afterwards arrived three Israelites together from the same city, apparently willing to receive Christianity; one of these was son of the brother, already mentioned, of the first visitor. " They were received with kindness, and instructed in many things of which their rabbis were ignorant:" and when taught the history of Christ, they all paid to his image the same adoration as their entertainers did. Some books being given them in the Chinese language, such as, " A Compendium of Christian Faith," and others of the same nature, they read them, and carried them home at their return.

They described their congregation as on the brink of extinction, partly from the decay of their national language, and partly because their chief had lately died at a very advanced age, leaving for his hereditary successor a son, very young, and very little versed in the peculiarities of their religion.

These personages readily fell in with several opinions of the missionaries. Trigaut tells us that they expressed a desire for pictures as helps to devotion, to be in their synagogue and private oratories, particularly for pictures of Jesus. They complained of the interdiction from slaughtering animals for themselves, which, if they had not transgressed recently upon the road, they must have perished with hunger. They were likewise ready to renounce the rite of circumcision on the eighth day, which their wives and the surrounding Heathen denounced as a barbarous and cruel practice. And they held out the expectation, that inasmuch as Christianity offers relief in such matters, it would be easily adopted among their people. Yet the author gives no account of any consequent conversions. He passes on abruptly from this subject of *Jewish filth* to relate the progress of *Christian truth* in China.

It appeared, on further inquiry, that the Chinese comprise under the one designation, *Hwuy-hwuy*, the three religions of Israelites, Mohammedans, and the Cross-worshippers, descendants of early Syrian Christians, subsisting in certain provinces, but occasionally distinguishing them thus:—

1. The Mohammedans, as the *Hwuy* abstaining from pork.
2. The Israelites, as the *Hwuy* who cut out the nerves and sinews from their meat; and,

3. The Cross-worshippers, who refuse to eat of animals which have an undivided hoof; which latter restriction, it was said, the Israelites there did not observe.

Julius Aleni, after the death of Ricci, being a Hebrew scholar, visited Kae-fung-foo about the year 1613, but found circumstances so much changed from some cause or other, that although he entered the synagogue and admired its cleanliness,[1] they would not withdraw the curtains which concealed the sacred books.

In Nan-king Semmedo was informed by a Mohammedan, that in that city he knew of four families of Jews who had embraced the religion of the Korân, they being the last of their race there, and their instructors having failed as their numbers diminished.

Indeed, the visitors from Kae-fung-foo had before assured Ricci, in Pe-king, that the same cause would soon reduce them to the alternative of becoming Heathens or Mohammedans.

However, Semmedo, writing in 1642, consoled himself with the hope that whereas a Christian church had been recently erected in that city, the congregation of the synagogue

[1] "If any synagogue can be free from uncleanness."—Semmedo.

would rather receive Christianity, which, besides the consideration of being the truth, is most nearly allied to their own religion.

The Mohammedans of Nan-king he described as a motley collection from various nations and æras of settlement; one of whom had surprised him by conversing about David, Abraham, Isaac, and Jacob, pronouncing these names very distinctly. He compared their condition to that of the Jews while in Spain, they being mostly merchants or physicians, only held in higher consideration than the Spanish Jews had been: inasmuch as in China the public honours are open to all aspirants.

Such was the amount of intelligence received in Europe concerning that remote off-shoot of Israel up to the middle of the seventeenth century. Christendom was not unconcerned at the discovery; China itself was but a newly-opened mine for European research; the indistinct glimpses afforded by Marco Polo in the thirteenth century were indeed extending into broader fields of vision, by means of the obedient zeal of Romanist missionaries. But when Xavier, expiring within sight of China, before admission was conceded to Christianity, prayed for its conversion with his latest accents, and when Valignano so frequently turned his looks from Macao towards the prohibited land, exclaiming, "O rock, rock, when wilt thou open?" they were not aware that within that strong solidity was to be found a relic of the peculiar nation who are everywhere witnesses of the "goodness and the severity of God."

The devout rejoiced at this fresh demonstration of Scripture truth respecting the scattered yet guarded race; the philosophical marvelled at the fact of a Mosaic people so ancient as to be ignorant of the denomination Jew, emigrants out of empires now long since extinct, into a very different phasis of civilization, but preserved with their old language and religion even to these days; and, moreover, that with so slight efforts made, these should be known to exist at four various points, containing a line of seven hundred miles, viz., from Pe-king to Hang-chow-foo.

But, perhaps, no class of men felt greater concern in the event than the laborious biblical critics of that time. To them the finding of some of that nation "to whom were committed the oracles of God," yet supposed to be of too ancient a separation to be cognizant of either the Samaritan, Septuagint, or Masoretic texts of the Old Testament, yet still guarding their copies of the law of Moses, was a circumstance most pregnant with hopeful interest, and the more a matter of anxiety as these Israelites were represented as almost ceasing to subsist, and there was great possibility that with the failure of Hebrew reading, consequent on the adoption of a novel creed, the manuscripts themselves might be suffered to perish. The subject was referred to in the Prolegomena (iii. § 41) of Walton's Polyglott Bible, and in the Preface to Jablonski's Hebrew Bible (§ 38), and further information as to the text of the Chinese copies of the Pentateuch was ardently desired.

A fuller account was afterwards received from Father Gozani, dated Kae-fung-foo, November, 1704, and published in 1707.[1] During this interval of more than sixty years' residence in the same city, with the only known synagogue in China, no intercourse had taken place between the missionaries and them, beyond one visit from Rodriguez de Figueredo, and another from Christian Enriquez, but who had shown no curiosity to inspect the Hebrew books, and had made no report on the subject to their

[1] In "Lettres édifiantes et curieuses."—Recueil vii.

superiors; the fact that they had made any visit was only learned by Gozani from the people of the synagogue. It is true that the Jesuits had found abundant occupation in their direct duties, in political intrigues, and in disputes with their rivals of the monkish orders, but for these latter employments the wise and the learned in Europe had but little cause to thank them.

From the communication of Gozani, it appears that in 1702 he had intended to visit the *Taou-kin-keaou*,[1] i.e., "the sect who cut out the sinew," as the Israelites were expressively designated, but was deterred by some imaginary obstacles, and by the real difficulty in his ignorance of the Hebrew language, but had resumed the task two years afterwards in obedience to instructions sent from Rome. He commenced by advancing certain civilities; in return they visited him; and then he proceeded to their synagogue (Le-pae-sze), the distance being only that of a few streets, where he found them assembled. They showed him their religious books, and even led him to the most sacred part of the edifice, to which only the rabbi

[1] The Chinese characters for these words are given at the commencement of this book.

(Chang-keaou) has right of access. With great politeness they gave him all the explanations he requested as to their Scriptures, their history, and their religious ceremonies. On the walls he perceived inscriptions both in Chinese and Hebrew: these they permitted him to copy, and he despatched the copies with his letter to Rome. The whole reception testified that the unfriendliness of the last half century between the neighbours was not attributable to the Israelite community.

The curiosity of Europeans being only the more excited from this narrative, as there still remained much to learn, at the instance of Souciet, who was compiling a large work upon the Bible, the missionaries Gozani, Domenge, and Gaubil, were successively directed to procure additional particulars on the subject, which they did. Domenge sketched a plan of the synagogue, and Gaubil copied afresh the inscriptions upon its walls. Shortly after the last of these visits, in 1723, the missionaries were expelled from that province by the Emperor Yong-ching.

An effort was afterwards made by the celebrated Kennicott, of Oxford, to obtain a collation of their Scriptures with our copies, when Sir F. Pigou, being on his way to Canton, carried out for him a printed Hebrew Bible of Amsterdam edition; but the only result has been a letter received in 1769, from a friend there, promising to exert himself for the purpose, and stating that the titular bishop of the province was willing to render his assistance.

The learned Tychsen, upon two later occasions, in 1777 and 1779, forwarded letters to friends in Batavia, addressed to the synagogue of Kae-fung-foo, but no information has been returned as to their having even reached China.

In 1815, the year previous to the last embassy from England to the Celestial Empire, some Jews of London had despatched a letter in Hebrew to Canton for this synagogue. It was conveyed thence by a travelling bookseller of the Ho-nan province. He delivered it at Kae-fung-foo, to a person whom he found to understand the letter perfectly, and who promised to answer it in a few days, but the bearer taking alarm at a rumour of civil war, left the place without waiting for the reply.[1]

The recent missionaries from England have

[1] Journal of the Embassy to China. By Henry Ellis. 1817.

learned nothing concerning this colony, only in 1816 Dr. Morrison heard of them from a Mohammedan near Pe-king,[1] as subsisting in Kae-fung-foo under their old name of "the religion of cutting out the sinew," an appellation so appropriately Jewish, that no other people than descendants of Jacob could even assign a reason for its origin, if they were to assume the name for any purpose.

Proceeding, then, from the information given by the Jesuits already mentioned, the account in the following chapters of the synagogue, Scriptures, inscriptions, &c., must be understood only of Kae-fung-foo, and upon the statements there detailed must be based the after-inquiry, as to whether the people are Jews or Israelites, that is, whether emigrants from the Assyrian captivity or the Roman dispersion.

[1] Davis's Chinese. Vol. I., p. 15.

## CHAPTER II.

### THE SYNAGOGUE.

The first report made concerning the house for Divine worship of the Hebrews in Kae-fung-foo was meagre in the extreme. Aleni visited there, and the attendants, for some temporary and unexplained reason, refused to draw the curtains which concealed the sacred volumes. He described the building as very handsome, and carefully kept.

The early missionaries, Ricci, Figueredo, and Enriquez, appear to have been absorbed in the stupendous task placed before them—that of converting unknown millions of Heathen to the discipline of the Roman Church. They were, probably, men of robust mental character and untiring industry, fitted for rougher duties than the pursuits of a learned leisure; such, indeed, is the prevailing tone of their correspondence. They were unacquainted with the Hebrew language and Jewish customs, both of which their early education had trained them to despise. Gozani, being one of the same stamp, while obeying singly the urgent instructions from his General, in respect to the Jewish colony of Kae-fung-foo, he had the good sense and honesty to write down exactly what his eyes and ears witnessed; yet with a proper degree of prudence, he himself prescribed the difference to be observed between the narration of what he heard and of what he saw.

But the intelligence resulting from the visits made between 1712 and 1723, is far more circumstantial in details, which Domenge and Gaubil, being Hebrew scholars, were able to elicit by propounding suitable questions. In giving a summary of their letters, and of the prior one from Gozani, out of Brotier, it may be well, until further knowledge is gained, to continue in the description his use of the present tense.

The whole place of worship occupies a space of between three and four hundred feet in length, by about one hundred and fifty in breadth, comprising four successive courts, advancing from the east to the synagogue itself at the extreme west.

The first court has in its centre " a large, noble, and beautiful arch" (Pae-fang), bearing a golden inscription in Chinese, dedicating the locality to the Creator and Preserver of all things. There are also some trees interspersed.[1]

The second court is entered from the first, by a large gate with two side doors, and two wickets beside them. Its walls are flanked to the north and south by dwellings for the keepers of the edifice.

The third court has the same kinds of entrance from the second as that has from the first. In its centre stands an arch like that in the first court. Upon the walls, between trees, are marble tablets (Pae-wăn), with inscriptions in Chinese. Part of this court is flanked by commemorative chapels: that on the south,[2] in memory of an Israelite mandarin named Chao, the judge of a city of second degree, who formerly rebuilt the synagogue after its destruction by fire: that on the north, in memory of him who erected all the present edifice. There are also some reception rooms for guests.

The fourth court is parted in two by a row of trees. Half way along this line stands a great

[1] Probably stinted to a dwarf size, by an art in which the Chinese take great delight.

[2] At the door of this chapel, or cell, is a figure of some animal, upon a pedestal; but what animal it was intended to represent, exceeded the ability of Domenge to tell.

brazen vase for incense, at the sides of which are placed two figures of lions, upon marble pedestals; and at the westward sides of these lions are two large brazen vases, containing flowers. Adjoining the northern wall is a recess, in which the nerves and sinews are extracted from animals slain for food. The second division of this court is an empty space, with a "hall of ancestors" (Tsoo-tang) at each of its sides to the north and south. In these they venerate, at the vernal and autumnal equinoxes, the worthies of the Old Testament history, after the Chinese manner, but having merely the name of the person upon each tablet, without his picture. The only furniture these contain are a great number of censers; the largest one in honour of Abraham, and the rest, of Isaac, Jacob, the twelve sons of Jacob, Moses, Aaron, Joshua, Ezra, and others, both male and female. In the open space between these chapels, they erect their annual booths of boughs and flowers, at the Feast of Tabernacles.

Then occurs the synagogue itself, a building of about sixty feet by forty, covered by a fourfold and handsome roof, having a portico with a double row of four columns, and a balustrade before it.

Within this edifice, the roofs (as usual in Chinese domestic architecture) are sustained by rows of pillars besides the walls. In the centre of all is " the throne of Moses,"[1] a magnificent and elevated chair, with an embroidered cushion, upon which they place the book of the law while it is read. Over this a dome is suspended; and near it is the Wăn-suy-pae, or tablet, with the Emperor's name in golden characters, enclosed within a double line of scroll-work. This, however, is surmounted by the inscription, in Hebrew letters of gold:—

    HEAR, O ISRAEL:
  THE LORD OUR GOD IS ONE LORD.
    BLESSED BE THE NAME
  OF THE GLORY OF HIS KINGDOM
    FOR EVER AND EVER.[2]

After this, a triple arch bears the following inscription, likewise in Hebrew:—

  BLESSED BE THE LORD FOR EVER.
THE LORD IS GOD OF GODS, AND THE LORD:
  A GREAT GOD, STRONG AND TERRIBLE.[3]

Then a large table, upon which are placed

---

[1] Was the Moses' seat in Matt. xxiii. 2, merely a figurative term?

[2] See Appendix A.

[3] See Appendix B.

six candelabra in one line, with a great vase for incense, having handles, and a tripod-standing, half-way along the line. These candelabra are in *three* different forms, and bear *three* different kinds of lights. Those nearest the vase bear torches, the next on each side have candles, and those at the extremities, ornamental lanterns. Near this table is a laver for washing hands.

Lastly, the Beth-el, or *Teën-tang* (house of heaven), square in outward shape, but rounded within. Into this none but the rabbi may enter during the time of prayer. Here, upon separate tables, stand twelve rolls of the law, corresponding to the tribes of Israel, besides one in the centre in honour of Moses, each enclosed in a tent of silken curtains. On the extreme western wall are the tablets of the Ten Commandments, in golden letters of Hebrew. Beside each of these tablets is a closet containing manuscript books, and in front of each closet, a table, bearing a vase and two candelabra.

The congregation when assembled for devotion are separated from the Beth-el by a balustrade, some standing in recesses along the walls. Against a column is suspended a calendar for the reading of the law.

Such is the edifice in which the children of Israel at Kae-fung-foo worshipped God within the last century. Gozani affirms it to be the only synagogue remaining in the empire. If this be true, that of Hang-chow-foo, mentioned by the first visitor to Ricci, must have shared the fate of that in Nan-king, as related to Semmedo.

Some writers have regarded this as rather a temple than a synagogue, but without sufficient reason, for the special characteristics of a temple are decidedly wanting. In China, as elsewhere, it may be truly asserted in the Hebrew Liturgy, that the worshippers have neither altar nor offering.[1] The homage paid to ancestors may partake somewhat of a sacrificial nature, but it is carefully dissevered from even local association with the adoration paid to Almighty God. The candelabra, the laver,

[1] "Lord of the universe, while the temple remained, if a man sinned he brought an offering and made atonement for himself; but now, because of our iniquities, we have neither sanctuary nor altar, nor offering, nor priest to atone for us, there is nothing left us but the commemoration of them. O may that be our expiation, and we will render the prayers of our lips instead of our offerings." —Morning Service.

the solitude of the rabbi in the Beth-el, and his use of incense there, as well as in the courts, together with the courts themselves, these suggest clear reminiscences of the Jerusalem Temple, but they do not prove that in China there has ever existed a rival temple to that of "the city which the Lord did choose, to put his name there," as was erected by Onias and his colony in Egypt,[1] or by the Samaritans at Gerizim.

It does not resemble the great synagogues of Amsterdam, Leghorn, or those of the Gallician province in Poland, on which considerable wealth has been lavished; still less does it copy the modesty of the primitive synagogues, in which the people assembled to hear the law and haphtorah, to recite the "eighteen blessings," or to join in some very simple form of supplication; but the very dissimilarity attests the high antiquity of this community's seclusion.

Among their religious forms and customs, may be enumerated the putting off of shoes on entering the house of prayer, and wearing a blue head-dress while there (a circumstance by

[1] Josephus Ant., xiii. 3, and Wars, vii. 10.

which the Heathen distinguish them from the Mohammedans, who wear white). In reading the law, the minister covers his face with a transparent veil of gauze, in imitation of Moses, who brought the law to the people with his face covered, and wears a red silk scarf, depending from the right shoulder and tied under the left arm. By his side stands a monitor to correct his reading, if necessary, who is likewise attended by a monitor. The prayers are chanted, but without musical instruments. The congregation wear no *talith* or garment of fringes during the service. They observe circumcision, passover, tabernacles, the rejoicing of the law, and, perhaps, the Day of Atonement, for it is said that on one day of the year they fast and weep together in the synagogue. They keep the Sabbath quite as strictly as do the Jews in Europe. They make no proselytes, and never marry with Gentiles. They use their sacred books in casting lots, and their literary men pay the same homage to the memory of Kung-foo-sze (Confucius) as their neighbours do. They never pronounce the ineffable name of God, but say *Etunoi* (*Adonai*), and in writing Chinese they render that name by Teën (heaven), just as the Chinese do, instead of *Shang-te* (Lord above), or any other ancient appellation of the Deity.[1]

They have no formulary of belief, but hold to the unity of God, and to the doctrines of heaven, hell, a sort of purgatory, the resurrection of the dead, the day of judgment, and the hierarchies of angels.

Of the Lord Jesus Christ they had never heard, only of one Jesus a son of Sirach. They expect Messiah, and frequently repeat the words of dying Jacob, " I have waited for thy salvation, O Lord."[2] To the question, what they understood by salvation, they made no

---

[1] Gozani and others referred to this substitution, in the controversy as to whether the Chinese adore the material heaven or the Person who is its Creator. The Jesuits contended that if Jews could conscientiously employ the word *heaven* to denote *God*, that sufficiently indicates the sense in which the Gentiles understand the term. They also appealed to Luke xv. 18, and 2 Macc. vii. 11, on the same side, as well as to the common use of the word *heaven* in the Talmud. It is curious to have Israelites called in to decide a point between the contrary decisions of Popes Innocent X., and Alexander VII. At length it became usual for the missionaries to adopt the designation Teën Choo (heaven's Lord).

[2] Gen. xlix. 18.

reply. When shown a crucifix in the mission-church they regarded it with no symptoms of displeasure, from which Brotier concludes that they know nothing of the Talmudic prejudice against "the Crucified," but it would seem that if they have no canonical Talmud with its Agadoth, they have some ridiculous legends of old tradition. "They related to me," says Gozani, "such foolish tales" (mingled with even the law of Moses), "that I could scarcely refrain from laughing." And in another place, " They spoke to me about heaven and hell in a very senseless manner."

Their alienation from idolatry is particularly striking, after so long an exposure to the superstitions of the country, guided as these are by Imperial influence. They refuse to take an oath in an idol temple; and the conspicuous inscriptions upon the walls and arches proclaim their steadfastness in this matter, even upon that delicate point of the Emperor's name, which in the synagogue they have surmounted by the most significant of possible warnings against confounding any reverence whatever with that due to the "blessed and only Potentate."

Nor must we omit to remark their interesting practice of praying westwards, towards Jerusalem. Many large bodies of Christians pray eastwards, from a feeling in favour of mere Orientation; but when we find European Jews praying eastwards, and their brethren in China turning to the west, both towards one intermediate locality, that one must be the station which an ancient psalmist considered "above his chief joy." "If I forget thee, O Jerusalem, let my right hand be forgetful."[1] And it must have been westward that Daniel turned when "his windows being open in his chamber toward Jerusalem, he kneeled upon his knees three times a-day, and prayed and gave thanks before his God, as he did aforetime,"[2] for he remembered the prophetic prayer of Solomon, "If they shall bethink themselves in the land whither they were carried captives, and repent, and make supplication unto thee . . . . . and pray unto thee *toward their land* which thou gavest unto their fathers, *the city* which thou hast chosen, and *the house* which I have built for thy name: then hear thou their prayer and their supplication in heaven thy dwelling-place, and maintain their cause."[3]

[1] Ps. cxxxvii.   [2] Dan. vi. 10.   [3] 1 Kings viii. 48, 49.

## CHAPTER III.

### SCRIPTURE AND LITERATURE.

THE writings of a people are in most cases interesting, as being the expression of that people's intelligence and sentiment—the product of their previous mental formation: but the Hebrew standard writings are the original mould in which the feelings and thoughts of its subjects are cast. And the sense of Divine authority to which the mind is by them subdued, tends in like manner to guard their own integrity. The sacred law is preserved in order to be obeyed, and the obedience thus rendered ensures its perpetual correctness.

The Lord of the new covenant has declared, that " till heaven and earth pass, one jot or one tittle shall in nowise pass from the law till all be fulfilled;"[1] and the Hebrew scribes have been everywhere and always careful that not one *jod*, or any one small indication of the sense of a word should be lost or changed.

Aware of this inflexibility, both the friends

[1] Matt. v. 18.

and impugners of Divine revelation were desirous to ascertain to what extent the separated Israelites in China possessed a text of the Bible conformable to ours; and the discoveries made there have served to establish the previous hopes of all who founded their expectations for eternity upon the Word of God.

As we have already seen, the synagogue of Kae-fung-foo possesses thirteen copies of the law, kept within coverings of silk. These are denominated the *Tă-king*, or Temple-Scripture. The rolls measure about two feet in length, and are rather more than one foot in diameter.

Besides these, there is in the Beth-el a large number of nearly square books (not rolls), of about seven inches by four or five, some new, others very old; but all much neglected, and lying in confusion. The people classified them nominally, as follows:—

1. *Tă-king*, in fifty-three books, each containing one section of the law, for the Sabbath-days.

2. *Tsin-soo*, or supplementary books; called, also, Ha-foo-ta-la, or Haphtorah. These are portions of Joshua, Judges, Samuel, Kings, and the Prophets.

3. Historical books, viz.:—Esther, Ezra,

Nehemiah, Chronicles (four or five of the first chapters), and the two first books of Maccabees, called Mattathi, the latter whole, but not in good condition.

4. *Keang-chang*, or the Expositors. These are much defaced, and have lost their titles. The brief leisure of the missionaries did not allow of a close examination into these books, their attention having been especially directed to the law of Moses.

5. *Le-pae*, the ritual or ceremonial books, about fifty in number, and slightly differing in shape from the rest. One of these bears on its cover the title, " The Perpetual Afternoon-Service."

Such is the best account that can be made out of the varied lists given us, of the books in that synagogue; all of which, however, can be shaped into the above form, by allowing the easy supposition that the missionaries were unfamiliar with the Jewish Haphtorah and Ritual; had they not been so, they would not have founded upon these portion-books so melancholy a narrative of the deficiency of Scripture in Kae-fung-foo, nor would the Europeans[1] have

---

[1] Brotier, Grosier, Calmet, and Kœgler,—the latter a better mathematician than Hebraist.

followed one after another in the same track, detailing exactly how much each book of the Prophets was mutilated; when, in fact, these small books were never intended to afford the whole of each prophecy, nor even the selections from each, in a regular sequence. The Portions are chosen as harmonizing in sentiment or doctrine with the section of the law for the particular week: and while the people exhibited these as their books of the synagogue, it is not impossible that they had elsewhere the complete rolls of the Prophets. Upon this view it becomes clear why Gaubil could not find Isaiah vii. 14, when they, having asked him to read them some Hebrew, he wished to fix their attention on that passage: he would have been equally unsuccessful in seeking for the chapter liii.

It is said that the books of Job, Proverbs, Song of Solomon, Ecclesiastes, Ruth, and Lamentations, are missing. The four last would have been found, if sought for at the end of Esther; which, together with the two first, and the list given us as the historical books, exactly make up the class usually called the *Kethubim*, or writings.

In this class ought to be found the Psalms;

but the name of David is placed along with Samuel and Kings: however, as these books were not at all inspected, it is reasonable to conclude that only the history of David was meant, and that the *Tehillim,* or Psalms, are in their proper place.

It is also said, that the book of Ezekiel is entirely lost. If so, we cannot identify the *Tsin-soo,* or, *Ha-foo-ta-la,* with Haphtorah, in which there are several portions from Ezekiel; but on Gozani's first visit, the people in the synagogue related to him the vision of the resurrection of dry bones in the valley, which very subject is in the Sephardim Haphtorah.[1] It may therefore be doubted that the recorded visions and denunciations of the son of Buzi, are lost in China. This portion is either in their Haphtorah or in a volume of Ezekiel; and although from the calamities to which the synagogue has at various times been exposed, some of their books may be lost, and others neglected, the Jews in Kae-fung-foo certainly possess in full their law, their Haphtorah, and ritual.

Some idea may be formed of the jealousy with which their Scriptures are kept, from the resistance made to all the entreaties and

[1] It is not in that of the German and Polish Jews.

tempting offers made for obtaining a transcript from any of them, or for permitting the visitors to copy for themselves. In Gozani's first letter, it was stated, that "all these books are preserved with greater care than gold or silver." And it was afterwards learned that they have a rule among them, "never to show their Scriptures to the black people."[1] During eight months' residence there, all the efforts of Domenge were fruitless to procure leave to copy the books of Maccabees, as an appendix to his Hebrew Bible.[2] One Ngai-ven, promised for a certain sum to get for him a volume of the

[1] This term was understood to denote all who eat swine's flesh; but in later times we know that "black-heads" is a familiar appellation throughout the country for the native Chinese.

[2] The Second Book of Maccabees has not been known to exist in Hebrew among any other people. It has been commonly regarded as a Greek compendium of a Greek history, written by one Jason, of Cyrene.

The first book was seen in its original Chaldaic Hebrew, by St. Jerome, under the title of "The Sceptre of the Prince of the sons of God;" but no such a text has been mentioned from that time until, as above, in the eighteenth century.

That these are found in China, is in some degree confirmed by the mention likewise made to Gozani, of Judith, and of Jesus the son of Sirach, which books were formerly extant in Chaldee.

*Tsin-soo*, but his attempt to extract it from the Beth-el being detected, he was made to replace it, and was rebuked with the proverb, " He who sells his Scripture sells his God." Another, named Kao-ting, having made a similar promise, demanded openly of the rabbi the beautifully-written manuscript of the law, which he had inherited from his late uncle, and had deposited in the synagogue: he too was rebuked, and retired with shame.

In explanation of these anecdotes it is to be observed, that books of Hebrew writing are scarcely ever kept in private dwellings: and it is said, that when a rich man presents a copy of the law to the synagogue, the merit of the gift is rated so high, as to supersede all necessity for public devotion during the remainder of his life: he seldom again attends Divine worship.

Information was received that a manuscript of the law of Moses existed in a certain temple at Pe-king, where the Government had secured copies of the sacred books used by all religions in the empire. The Jesuits, therefore, procured a license to search for this treasure, but nothing of the kind was found, only some ancient writing, in Syriac. They suspected that the keeper of the temple had been induced to conceal the real object of their investigation, while exhibiting that which in some degree resembled it. Attempts were afterwards made to institute a fresh scrutiny of that library, but in vain. A Christian Tartar, to whom the missionaries showed their Hebrew Bible, declared that in that temple at Pe-king, he had seen books in the same character of writing, of whose contents or antiquity he knew nothing, only that one of them was called *Torah*.

At length Gaubil concluded a bargain for a transcript of the law; but before it could be completed, the missionaries were expelled from the province.

From the direct statements, and from unintentional glimpses contained in the missionary correspondence, several of the first Oriental scholars in Europe have framed dissertations upon the antiquity and consequent value of the manuscripts in Kae-fung-foo.

It is known from ancient inscriptions upon the walls of the synagogue, that in 1462 their loss of books by an inundation of the Hwang-ho, was supplied from Ning-po and Ning-kea; that being again deprived of books by a fire at the close of the sixteenth century, a roll of the law was purchased from a Mohammedan at Ning-keang-chow, in Shen-se, who had received it by legacy from a dying Israelite at Canton, recommended as a relic of great antiquity. Possessing this, they made from it several copies.

It is also known, that in 1642, the synagogue again suffered from an inundation, which destroyed or carried off twenty-six volumes of different kinds, notwithstanding great efforts for their recovery.

Now there is one manuscript kept apart from the rest, in this synagogue, held in peculiar veneration, and named in honour of Moses. It was so honoured in 1704, while it bore serious marks of injury caused by the water, the writing in several places being almost effaced. It has been supposed, with much apparent reason, that this is identical with the Canton manuscript procured from the Mohammedan after the conflagration, and with that which the visitor to Ricci, about 1604, described as being four or five hundred years old. This, therefore, constitutes a very prominent object of regard in connexion with the Chinese Jews. The earlier Ning-po manuscript must have perished in the flames.

But in the closets there may also be books of considerable antiquity, as it does not appear that all were lost in 1642. One small page has particularly arrested the attention of the curious. At the end of the section-book *Bereshith*, there is a list of rabbis, with a date, which De Sacy has shown, by a careful computation,[1] to correspond with A.D. 1620, i.e., twenty-two years before the last inundation; although he considers it very probable that this leaf may not now be in its original place, but be a fragment of some lost manuscript, since it is known that after this calamity, a great number of loose leaves and detached parts of books were bound into one thick volume.

This record is in Hebrew, mixed with several Persian words in Hebrew character. The learned Olave Gerhard Tychsen interprets it as follows, in a letter to C. T. Murr,[2] A.D. 1799:—

"In the city anciently (called) Pin-lignan,[3] the divine city, by Divine help. The law of

[1] See Appendix C.
[2] Diarii litterarii II., 304. See Appendix D.
[3] Or, according to De Sacy, "In the city anciently (called) Pien-leang, the divine city, by Divine help, the law of fifty-three sections, contains, O Israel, true words," &c.

fifty-three sections, ordained for Israel, the word of God, the faithful King.[1]

" This beginning of the law was written in the year 1933, in the month Ab, on the first day of the week, and twelfth day of the month.

" The law was completed in the year 1937, in the month Iyar, on the fourth day of the week, on the twelfth day of the month.

" Our master, our rabbi, R. Jacob, son of Abishai, the son of R. Eldad the scribe, and melammed (teacher), finished this.

" R. Shadai, son of R. Jacob, revised it.

" R. Mordecai, son of Simeon Besprisht, and R. Akiba, son of Aaron the son of Ezra, subscribed it.

" The youth (student) Simhhah, son of Joshua the son of Joseph the exalted, gave it[2] as a free-will offering.

" R. Jacob, son of Reuben the son of Buzi.

" Mordecai, son of Benjamin the son of Buzi.

---

[1] Tychsen believes this word אֹמֶן to represent a Talmudic phrase (Sanhed. III., i. 1), "the faithful king;" and thence concludes (indè palàm fit) that in China the Jews are not Karaites but Talmudists.

[2] By the rendering of Tychsen the gift was from R. Akiba, but the words as we have them do not sanction this meaning.

"Blessed shalt thou be when thou comest in, and blessed shalt thou be when thou goest out.[1]

"And he was very rich in cattle (and) in silver.[2]

"I have waited for thy salvation, O Lord."[3]

The commencement of this document does seem to assert that it belonged to a roll of the whole law, rather than to one section only.

Thus much for the external description and history of these manuscripts. The internal examination is, at least, a subject of equal importance.

It was from the first ascertained that the books of the law of Moses were named, as with us, from the opening words in each book, as *Bereshith*, *Shemoth*, &c. Ricci's convert and Gozani had learned thus much, although unacquainted with Hebrew. Also, that the law was read in fifty-three instead of fifty-four sections. The latter fact was remarked afterwards by Domenge, who found in the week of tabernacles

---

[1] Deut. xxviii. 6.

[2] Genesis xiii. 2. The name Abraham is omitted, as also the words, " and in gold." The allusion is to some living person, and certainly the metal, gold, is very scarce in China.

[3] Genesis xlix. 18.

that they read the section *Wa-yelek*, having thus united the Masoretic fifty-second and fifty-third into one.

The people showed no desire to collate their Scriptures with the European text, only in one instance. Gozani with his Latin Bible, and the rabbi with his *Bereshith* (" for so they call the book of Genesis"), compared the names and ages of persons in the genealogy from Adam to Noah. In these they found a perfect accordance, particularly he observed that they agreed in Gen. xi. 12, where the name *Cainan* is introduced by the Septuagint, and in Luke iii. 36; but is omitted in our Hebrew, and consequently in the Vulgate. They also compared, with the same result, several other names and ages in other books of the law.

Domenge having been instructed from Rome to collate the Hebrew of the following passages in the law, Gen. ii. 17; iii. 17; vii. 11; viii. 4, 7; the whole of chap. xi.; xiii. 3; xviii. 22; xxiii. 2; xxiv. 2; xxxiii. 4; and the whole of chapters xlvii., xlviii., and xlix.; in all of these he found the most entire correspondence. However, in Deut. xxxii. 25, instead of "destroy," their text has "devour," the letter שׁ being changed for א. It might be wished that Deut. xi. 29, and xxvii. 12, 13, had been examined with reference to the Samaritan text.

These Israelites were pleased with the interpretation given by Gaubil to the Lord's ineffable name, as implying a past, present, and future existence, and said that they had always perceived in it that signification.[1]

When asked for the meaning they attached to the word *Shiloh*, they remained silent for a time, but as soon as the visitor began to explain the sense attributed to it in the Christian Church, a youth who was present very deferentially requested leave to speak. He stated, that he recollected one of his great-uncles having formerly taught him that the word *Shiloh* contained a sacred mystery; written in this manner, the letters corresponding to the words.

ש = Great.
י = One.
ל = Descending.
ה = Man.

This he remembered, but he knew no more on the subject.

Gaubil was delighted with this information,

[1] See Appendix E.

as it seemed to corroborate a curious discovery he had made shortly previous. Being at Hankeow, he learned that the missionary there, Father Couteux, had under instruction a Chinese learned in antique modes of writing, and feeling persuaded that the word *Shiloh* was a word of mysterious or sacramental import among ancient nations, he showed to the catechumen (who was totally ignorant of Hebrew), that word in the perpendicular manner of Chinese writing, adopting the phonetic system required for foreign names, i.e., a sound or word for a letter, and the explication given was this:—

ש = Most High.
י = Lord.
ל = One.
ה = Man.

The partial coincidence is certainly striking, and if not the coinage of Oriental reverie in later times (for Cabalistic Jews are accustomed to revel in such modes of deduction), are somewhat confirmatory of the speculations which have deduced the Chinese population from an Egyptian original, and in so far tending to retrace the two traditions to a common origin in Egypt, where Abraham resided with a reputation of Divine inspiration after the promise of the world's redemption had been given him.

With regard to writing and reading among the Jews in Kae-fung-foo, it is stated that they are generally ignorant of the Hebrew language, although from the effect of constant repetition they read off the law with much fluency. For this ignorance they accounted by alleging a total loss of books on grammar (Too-king-pwan), and the cessation for two centuries of all arrivals of brethren from the west (Se-yïh).

From probably the same causes they have learned to read Hebrew with Chinese pronunciation; thus, though their written alphabet is precisely the same as with us, the consonants B, D, G, and R, are pronounced P, T, or Z, K, and L, and for the termination, הו, to a word they give a nasal sound, as (in Gen. i. 2), תהו ובהו, they read *Theohung-vo-peohung*. One of them writing his name, מתיתו, pronounced it *Manthi-iohung*.[1]

---

[1] The names of the five books of Moses they pronounced Pe-lesh-itze, She-meot-ze, Va-yi-ke-lo, Pe-me-ze-paul, and Te-ve-liim. The Prophets' names they read from the Bible of the missionaries, I-se-ha-ha, Ie-le-me-o-hung, Iu-en-a-ha, Mi-ca-ha, Na-hoo-am, Ha-pa-coo-ke, Se-pha-ne-o-ha, Ho-ko-e, and Se-ca-le-o. The Chronicles, Ti-

They seemed anxious to hear their visitors read with European pronunciation.

Although they admired the neatness of the printing, paper, and binding of the Hebrew Bible, they expressed no covetousness in that matter.

Their rolls of the law have no vowel points. When asked the reason of this, they replied, that the Lord uttered the words in too rapid a manner for Moses to insert them, but that they were afterwards supplied by the learned men in the west.

The *Tă-king* sections of the law are written in larger character than the rolls, and have vowel-points, stops, and accents, all of which are comprised under the general name *Siman* or marks. The accents are about the same as with us, only they write Athnahh, ˃; Merca, ˗; and Zakeph-gadol, t.

The subject of *Keri* and *Kethib* was quite new to them, and they knew of no "alteration by the Scribes" in Gen. xviii. 22.

The small or large letters occasionally met

ve-lé ha-ya-mim; Esther, Is-se-tha; and Mordecai, Mol-tho-gai.

Thus the vowels are, for Kholem, ue or eo; for Kamets, o; for Pathahh, broad ae; and i, as in French.

among words of Scripture they retain with scrupulous exactness, as in all other Hebrew texts, long after the reason of the variations has ceased to be understood. Thus in Gen. ii. 4, the ה of בהבראם is diminished, and in xxiii. 2, where the כ in ולבכתה did not appear small, the rabbi declared that it was and ought to be so. Also in xxxiii. 4, as in our printing, the word ישקהו has the six dots above it, with the first larger than the others.

The short line called *Rapheh* is employed in the rolls of the law above the בגדכפת letters, when these have no *Dagesh*.

With respect to the *Pethuhhah* and *Sethumah*, for either פפפ and ססס, or פ and ס, they leave no spaces, but insert in the margin either פ), or ס), or פס), yet very frequently the minor division is not regarded at all, as in the benediction of Jacob (Gen. xlix.), and these signs seldom occur in the same places as with us. Thus in the first section of the law they have only four divisions marked, viz., at the end of chap. i. 9; at the end of verse 26; at the end of chap. ii. 20; and of iii. 13.

The song of Moses in Deut. xxxii. is written in double columns.

In the rolls of the law the sections are not

always separated. Thus after "Noah," all the remainder of Genesis is marked לך לך, but the smallest subdivisions (Pesukim) are carefully observed, and are uniform with ours. Each book of the sections has the sum of these *Pesukim* given at its close: thus at the end of *Bereshith* is written קמו (146), and at the end of *Noah* is written קמג (143).

These books have their titles on the first page within a square of blue, green, or white[1] lines, as thus, בראשית, but the name is not repeated over each page, and the pages are not numbered with the letters of the alphabet, but with the full words, one, two, three, &c. The page contains about ten lines.

It is observed, that these manuscripts, both rolls and books, are not of parchment but of several folds of the thin Chinese paper pasted into one consistence,[2] and the Hebrews never employ Chinese pencils or ink for sacred purposes, but they split bamboo into pens, and

---

[1] Chinese paper is not white.

[2] Those who delight to trace the Chinese to the Egyptians, may find that this method was used by the latter people in preparing papyrus. See Wilkinson's "Manners and Customs of the Ancient Egyptians." iii. 148.

like the European Jews make annually at the feast of Tabernacles sufficient ink for the ensuing year.

It is stated, that they have written no books about themselves but one, which they keep and exhibit to the Gentiles whenever their religion is called in question.

This chapter may conclude with an explanation of the calendar of the ritual mentioned in chapter ii.[1] As it stands, being but ill-arranged, we find that there are five terms called *Mineah*, one corresponding to each of the books of Moses. This is shown by tracing a line from the word Genesis to the Mineah, א, from the word Exodus to the Mineah, ב, and so of the rest. The first, therefore, is read during the twelve sections of the law in Genesis; the second during the eleven in Exodus; the third during the ten in Leviticus, &c.

But the word *Mineah* can be nothing else than *Minhhah*, i.e., the afternoon service; changing one guttural letter for another, which we are warranted to do by the inscription upon the title-page of one of the *Le-pae* books, which, though it has been copied incorrectly in another of its letters, is correct in this guttural,

[1] See Appendix F.

the title being מנחה תמיד. Thus the afternoon-service, which in European liturgies is uniform throughout the year, is varied in China according to the book of the law which is read.[1]

But besides the *Minhhah* there are the terms *Moed Neumah* and *Muphtar Minhhah*. When Domenge inquired the signification of these he was unable to seize the meaning of the reply, owing to their Chinese pronunciation of Hebrew words, only he understood that the *Neumah* was a book in twelve parts, one of which was to be read on the first days of each short month (i. e., a month of twenty-nine days), or second days of each long month (thirty days), and that *Muphtar* is the title of a book appointed to be read on the fifteenth days of each short month, or sixteenth days of each long month.

Hence, De Sacy believes that as *Moed* is the Hebrew for "festival," and *Neumah* is the Persian for "new moon," that they have thus a variable form for celebrating the new moons,

---

[1] Is it possible that in this synagogue there is no service for the morning beyond reading the section of the law on the Sabbath? and no evening service whatever? The *Le-pae* books are not said to bear any title but *Minhhah*, and this calendar has no such terms as *Shahharith* or *Arabith*. No other calendar is known.

whereas in Europe that celebration is always the same.

*Muphtar Minhhah* is read at seasons of full moon; the latter of the two words determines the time to be afternoon, and the former signifies, "dismissal."[1]

This, too, is varied according to the alternate months; but for the full moon the Jews of Europe have no appointed prayer or thanksgiving, only they have a custom "to bless the brightness," as they express it. This they do from a notion that the continual providence of God is more discernible in the rotation of the moon's changes than in the sameness of the sun's appearance.

Whether the long and short months of the Chinese-Hebrew calendar correspond with those in these western parts we are not informed, but in the latter we have the new moons not only observed on the first days but also on the day which closes the preceding month; thus in one

[1] In literal signification the term applies very well to the Haphtorah portions, but with this idea the above description by no means coincides. Still it must be remembered that Domenge had great difficulty in comprehending the rabbi's meaning, which, therefore, he may have mistaken.

sense resembling the calendar in Kae-fung-foo, which allows a diversity of day according to the character of the month.

One more observation. Domenge describes the third of October, 1722, as being the twenty-third of the seventh month, according to the synagogue, and the octave of the "feast of tabernacles," the next day being the feast of "rejoicing for the law," when they carried the thirteen rolls of the law in a procession round the Beth-el, but there must be an error here. The law commands that the "feast of tabernacles" shall be kept upon the fifteenth day of the seventh month, its octave would thus occur on the twenty-second, and the "rejoicing for the law" upon the twenty-third. Either, therefore, he reckoned erroneously in the Christian calendar or in that of the synagogue, through a confusion in the long and short months.

## CHAPTER IV.

### INSCRIPTIONS, HISTORY, &c.

It is remarkable how entirely all Chinese books have contrived to omit the existence of the people under our consideration. The terms used by the latter for their exclusive designation, as *Kew-keaou*, the ancient religion; *Y-se-lo-yel keaou*, Israel's religion; *Taou-kin-keaou*, the religion of cutting out the nerves or sinews. These are not found in their dictionaries, and the geographical work in forty books upon Kae-fung-foo and its district, published in 1694, describes every edifice in the city with characteristic minuteness except the synagogue; every public inscription except those on the walls of that synagogue.[1] Yet these are the best records of its history known to survive the frequent devastations to which the community has been exposed.

[1] Memoires concernant les Chinois, par les Missionnaires de Pekin. Paris, 1791, tom. xv. p. 52. Also Deguignes' "Histoire Generale," i. 26, and Gutzlaff's "Three Voyages," p. 287.

The fortunes of the city have been greatly diversified. Before the Christian æra it was the capital of a petty kingdom named Wei. Under the Tsin and Han dynasties it was annexed to other districts. Its present appellation was bestowed in the middle of our third century; afterwards replaced by that of Peën-chow, but again resumed. Under the Woo-tae it was named Leang-chow; under the Kin, called Nang-kin; by the Mongol Tartars, named Peën-lang; and finally under the Ming, it recovered the ancient denomination of Kae-fung-foo.[1]

Its greatest prosperity was in the twelfth century, when, according to the 16th book of the *Kae-fung-foo-che*, the city was six leagues in circuit, approached by five roads bordered by willows and aspen-trees; one of these roads being reserved for persons of distinction, two for foot passengers, and two for carts of burden, &c. Its palaces, gardens, and government-houses are pourtrayed with great animation. This city has nevertheless suffered from inundation fifteen times; from general fires, six times; and has sustained eleven sieges.

[1] Th. Murr., from the "Atlas Sinensis" of Martini, pp. 59, 60.

It was in A.D. 1163 that the Israelites obtained leave from the Emperor Heaou-tsung, to erect there a synagogue.

In 1446 an inundation of the Hwang-ho (yellow river) destroyed the synagogue which had stood for nearly three hundred years, and many of their books perished.

In the beginning of the seventeenth century, under Wan-leih, the synagogue was consumed by fire, and all its books were burned.

And in 1642, in order to terminate the horrors produced by the siege of a rebel army, when human flesh was openly sold in the markets, and the garrison were served with rations of the same; the Imperialist commander opened the dykes of the river for the purpose of overwhelming at once both the enemy and the city. From this act the invaders suffered least, but in the city 100,000 persons[1] perished. It need hardly be added, that the synagogue shared the common fate.

These facts, and the traditions concerning the more remote history of these Hebrews, are chiefly gathered from the following four inscriptions in Chinese upon the marble tablets of the synagogue.

[1] Some say 200,000, but others 300,000.

I.

*(Erected by King-chong, a learned Israelite,*
A.D. 1444.)

"The author of the law of Israel was Abraham, the nineteenth from Adam.[1] This holy man lived 146 years after the beginning of the Chow[2] (dynasty). His law was transmitted to Moses, who received his book on Mount Sina, when he had fasted forty days and forty nights. He was always nigh unto heaven (God). In that book are fifty-three sections; its doctrine is nearly the same with that of the Chinese sages [here he produces traditions from each, which have great similarity], prescribing nearly the same rites for the worship of heaven (God), for ceremonials, fasting, prayer, and honouring the dead. Moreover, in the (Chinese) book Yi-king, are found vestiges of observing the Sabbath. Moses lived 613 years after the beginning of the Chow (dynasty). [Then in a

[1] This was their constant assertion. It is to be accounted for by the omission of Cainan from the genealogy. (See the preceding chapter.)
[2] Not the Chow empire of all China, but their earlier domination in the kingdoms now provinces.

reference to Ezra] he by exceeding diligence re-established and reformed the people."

Appended to the above is a statement that the synagogue was destroyed in the eleventh year of Ying-tsung (A.D. 1446), and most of the books spoiled by water, but that fresh books were supplied by Israelites from Ning-po and Ning-kea, one of whom named Yn, from Ning-po, brought in 1462 a complete copy of the law, by which they corrected what they had remaining. And that in the second year of Hung-che (A.D. 1490), the synagogue was rebuilt at the expense of Yeu-too-la.[1]

## II.

*(Erected by Tsu-tang, Treasurer of the province of Sze-chuen, in the fifteenth year of Hung-che.)*

"The law of Israel. Adam the first man was from Teën-chu[2] in the west. The Israelites have a law and tradition. The law is contained in five books, or fifty-three sections.

[1] Qu. Ventura?

[2] Gaubil says, that Chinese books mention five places under this name. The first near Medina, in Arabia, the others are in Tartary.

[Then follows a commendation of the law.] The Israelites worship heaven as we do: the author of their law was Abraham their father: Moses their legislator gave them his law. In the time of Han they settled in this country. In the year 20 of the lxvth cycle (A.D. 1163), they brought a tribute of Indian cloth to the Emperor Heaou-tsung.[1] Being well received they remained in Kae-fung-foo, which was then called Peën-lang. Then they were seventy Tsung[2] (i. e., surnames or clans). They built a synagogue, and in it laid up sacred books, which concern not only themselves but all men, kings and subjects, parents and children, the old and the young. Whosoever studies therein will perceive that their law differs but little from ours. Their summary is, to worship heaven, to honour parents, and to give due veneration to the dead. This people excelling in agriculture, in merchandise, in magistracies, and in

---

[1] Cotton cloth was first woven in China, near the end of our thirteenth century. "Morrison's View," &c.

[2] That Tsung denotes a clan, is seen from what Domenge was told, that in the seven Tsung then remaining there were a hundred families. A century earlier Ricci was informed of ten or twelve Tsung of Israelites subsisting in Kae-fung-foo.

warfare, are highly esteemed for integrity, fidelity, and strict observance of their religion. Their law was transmitted from Adam to Noah, from Noah to Abraham, from Abraham to Isaac, to Jacob, to the twelve tribes, to Moses, to Aaron, to Joshua, and to Ezra, who was a second lawgiver."

### III.

*(Erected* A. D. 1663, *the second year of Kanghe, by a Mandarin, afterwards Minister of State.)*

[After mention of Adam, Noah, Abraham, and Moses, he extols] " the virtue of Abraham, who adored the effective and preservative cause of all things, without any image or figure. Of the law which Moses received on Mount Sina there are thirteen copies, besides other books. The Israelites came to China in the time of the Chow (dynasty.)" [After praising their constancy in religion, he adds,] "They scarcely differ from us in the worship of heaven, in the duties of civil life, or in honouring the dead. The Sabbath was anciently observed by the Chinese. The Hebrew letters resemble the old Chinese."

[Then is related at length the inundation of

1642, in which the synagogue lost twenty-six of its volumes. Also is described the care taken in 1654 to revise, restore, and transcribe their books, with the names of persons who assisted in rebuilding the synagogue].

IV.

[This inscription is of the same subject-matter as the last; but has added the names of the seven Hebrew Tsung, then residing in Kae-fung-foo, viz., Tao, Kin, Che, Kao, Teman, Le, and Ngai.]

By these durable and respectable documents we are directed to two æras of this colony's arrival in China. The second of the tablets states, that " in the time of Han they settled in the land," i.e., between A.C. 205 and A.D. 220. The third affirms that they arrived in the time of the Chow, i.e., between A.C. 1122 and 249. And it deserves remark, that these two inscriptions, for whatever purpose, or from whatever motive, were set up by non-Israelites.

A third date has been deduced from the answer to Gaubil, in 1723, when he inquired of these how long they had been in the country, and they said, about 1650 years. Now this would coincide with the Roman overthrow of

Jerusalem, and be included in the dynasty of Han: but may it not denote the period of their coming to Kae-fung-foo? and as we know that their compatriots have resided and prospered in other parts of the empire, the latter may have been settlers from the prior dynasty of Chow.

It has been said that they are a remnant of the ten lost tribes; but there are no reasons for the supposition beyond the asserted ignorance of the denomination Jew, expressed by the first visitor to Ricci, and the fact that fragments of those broken tribes are really to be found in several parts of Central and Southern Asia.

But that the Hebrews in Ho-nan are Jews of the restoration from Chaldæa, is evident from the following considerations:—

1. The tablets speak of a tradition of the law from its origin to the time of Ezra, " the second lawgiver and reformer of the people;" a description which implies a knowledge of the re-establishment in Jerusalem.

2. They possess, besides some portions of the prophetical books written after the captivity of the ten tribes by Shalmaneser, a few verses of Daniel, and the book of Esther (whom they venerate under the title of " the great mother"), in which the word *Jew* occurs many times,

although the words *Israel* and *Israelite* are not found there at all.

3. Their Haphtorah (a selection dating only from the persecution by Antiochus Epiphanes, about A.C., 170) comprises portions out of prophets who lived in Jerusalem during the second temple, as Zechariah and Malachi.

4. They have adopted the Seleucidan æra of chronology.

5. In the list of rabbis annexed to the section-book, *Bereshith*, are found the titles, " our master, our rabbi," &c., which give it quite a Talmudic complexion: and they have Rabbinical rules for slaughtering.

6. The synagogue inscription over the Emperor's tablet, is a verse from Scripture, frequently repeated in Jewish liturgies to the present day.

The force of all the above reasons might indeed be abated, by taking into account, that for several centuries their sacred books, and some of their teachers, have reached them from another country in the west, and concluding that thus only may have been imported the later Scriptures and Jewish peculiarities. But this conclusion is entirely gratuitous, without evidence of even the lowest degree.

That this, however, is a very ancient off-shoot from the Jerusalem Jews, anterior, probably, to the incarnation of Christ, seems plain, from their ignorance of his name Jesus, that "which is above every name," until it was mentioned to them by the missionaries; perhaps, also, from their indifference towards the crucifix; from their freedom from Rabbinical despotism; and, above all, from those religious usages in which they differ from all Jews known elsewhere, such as reading the law through a veil, erecting a throne for Moses, together with their diversity in the sections of the law, and in their ritual of worship. But these will not lead us to declare their descent from the ten tribes.[1]

[1] The Abbé Sionnet, in 1837, published a memoir on the subject, which has been commended by eminent scholars; in which he contends for the earliest supposed migration of this people, and that from the following reasons:—

1. A comparison of Jewish history with that of China, under the dynasty of Chow.

2. The traditions to be found in Chinese works, written some centuries before the Christian æra, in which allusions are made to Paradise, the tree of knowledge of good and evil, the rainbow after the deluge, Noah's sacrifice, the woman changed to a statue, the seven years' famine, the manna with a pleasant taste, the rock which gave out

We have sufficient testimony of their similarity for enabling us to connect them with the families of Judah and Benjamin, every day before our eyes; and, at the same time, a sufficient discrepancy to prove that the two branches of the same people have been long without mutual intercourse.

Their own account of arrival thither is merely that their forefathers came from the west, probably by way of Khorassan and Samerkand, the main route of ancient commerce in that direction: and their use of Persian words has been connected with this circumstance.

A solitary glimpse into their middle-age history is found in an account of India and China, by two Mohammedan travellers of our

water when struck by a rod, the sun arrested by command of a chief, &c.

3. The Divine name in the Hebrew religion, being found in the Tao-te-king of Laou-sze, written six centuries before our æra.—See Appendix E.

But can the first of these be clearly established? and would not the second and third be answered by the great probability of Laou-sze having procured the Hebrew law in Assyria during the seventy years' captivity, at the same period with Pythagoras, the western philosopher?

ninth century,[1] who describe a rebel, named Bae-choo, taking Canton by storm, in A. D. 877, and slaughtering 120,000 of Mohammedans, *Jews*, Christians, and Parsees.

Their residence in the Celestial Empire seems to have partaken of the monotony and comfort of the native Chinese; and the tablets erected by Gentile neighbours in their very synagogue, open to the world, and challenging contradiction, bear witness to the esteem which this community in general has maintained, and the honours to which members of it have arrived in various pursuits of life.

There is much of pleasure in perceiving how freshly they retain the sentiment of their nationality, as we find them rehearsing to their visitors the leading events of scriptural record, particularly how they had formerly inhabited a country in the west which Joshua conquered after leaving Egypt, and traversing the Red Sea and Desert with their people, to the number of sixty *wan* (myriads); commemorating their ancestors, even though it be with Chinese modes of reverence—paying respect, even though by mistake, to the picture of Rebekah

[1] Translated by the Abbé Renaudot. Paris. 1718.

and her children; and, perhaps, not less exhibited by their attachment to the Hebrew language under circumstances of so much discouragement, and by the pleasure they showed in inviting the missionaries to read to them some Hebrew Scripture.

Had there been a visitor from Europe of the family of Abraham, we cannot doubt that he might have gathered information more ample and more definite respecting this colony, than that now in our possession. Not every Christian preacher is competent to succeed in such a task, even when no difficulties arise from adverse prejudice, or a want of facility in the standard language. And when we consider how greatly the dialects of the several Chinese provinces vary from each other in pronunciation, we can scarcely wonder that the Jesuits frequently complained of the replies to their questions being nearly unintelligible; just as those questions also may have been to the persons to whom they were addressed.

Fortunately, the Hebrew books and the Chinese inscriptions were not so liable to misinterpretation.

## CHAPTER V.

### REFLECTIONS.

We have by this time gained some clear ideas, to a certain extent, respecting the Ho-nan Jews, their worship, their Scriptures, and the antiquity of their settlement. But as we have found hints and traces of their brethren in other situations of China, as Nan-king, Ning-po, Hang-chow-foo, &c., it is to be hoped that future research will give us intimations of them in these localities, as well as new particulars of those in Kae-fung-foo. Meanwhile it is not likely that this subject will lose its interest among us There is a keen expectation in the minds of many, that at least some curious illustrations of the Bible history and principles will yet be met in that country.

Some students of the unfulfilled prophecies look towards China for the discovery of the ten tribes, and certainly, if it can be shown that they have ever existed there in a large community, the institutions of no other country would be so capable of preserving their integrity during the long elapsed term of their disappearance.

Others regard with reverence the glimpses occasionally revealed of antique Chinese traditions agreeing most strangely with the books of Moses, of which the following affords one instance:—

A cloth-manufacturer in Stockport lately brought some samples of a mixed cotton and woollen cloth to a house of the same trade in Leeds. The proprietor of the latter having no occasion for the goods, and remarking that the colours were mostly suited to Asiatic taste, suggested that they might be sent to China. It was answered, "They have been there already, and sold at a fair profit, but were returned in a few days, by the Hong merchants, who pronounced it contrary to their religion that animal and vegetable substances should be woven together and worn."

The resemblance of this to the precept in Levit. xix. 19, is perfect,—" neither shall a garment mingled of linen and woollen come upon thee;" but no trace of such a prohibition has been discovered among any other than these nations: yet what must have been the period when it obtained not only admission but religious sanction in China?[1]

Others, again, have traced considerable similitude in certain sayings of Chinese philosophers which have become familiar proverbs, with the Biblical proverbs of Solomon.

On the other hand, the tablets of the synagogue, as described in the last chapter, allude to the correspondence of feeling in the Chinese and the Israelites, on the subject of veneration due to parents living and deceased. Such a principle, indeed, has ever prevailed among the Jewish people. Not only is it enjoined under the most awful authority, but their teachers have constantly laboured to instil the sacred obligation. Josephus says,[2] " The law ordains that parents should be honoured immediately after God himself;" and the daily liturgy, in enumerating " the commandments,

[1] " Christian Lady's Magazine." 1842. Of course it is possible that warm imaginations may give weight to coincidences of exceeding tenuity ; such as the proportions of Noah's ark being the same as those of a Chinese junk : the wise men having come from the East to inquire for the infant King of the Jews : and the name, Shinar, being very like China.

[2] Cont. Ap. ii. 28.

which, when a man performs them, he enjoys the interest (of his reward) in this life, and the principal in the world to come," places first of all " the honouring of father and mother."

Connected with the above is the reverence paid to old age by each of these nations. The Hebrew law enjoins,[1] " Thou shalt rise up before the hoary head, and honour the face of the old man, and fear thy God; I am the Lord." Urging this lesson from the same motive, but with greatly inferior pathos, Josephus continues. " The law also says, that young men should pay due respect to every elder, since God is the eldest of all beings." And Chinese instructions of the kind are very well known.

In the matter of venerating the dead, it is still uncertain whether or not the Chinese carry it to the extent of adoration; but, like them, the Israelites in that country burn lamps before the names of their ancestors; and the sacrifices of incense, accompanied by a species of supplication, offered by the former at the parental graves at certain recurring periods, are nearly paralleled even among Jews in Europe and Palestine, when they visit the burial-places

[1] Levit. xix. 32.

upon the Day of Atonement, reciting the names of departed friends or relatives, and praying to them[1] according to a ritual called " The answer of the tongue." (Prov. xvi. 1.)

A recent missionary to the *Beni-Israel*, of Bombay, exclaimed, on seing them practise several idolatrous usages, " How like they are to the Heathen!" but instantly added, " yet how unlike!"[2] So there is and must be everywhere, an indelible line discerned between the people of Abraham and every other race; and however modified by Chinese associations and circumstances, the synagogue of Kae-fung-foo is quite Hebraic still.

[1] Dr. Jost's " Israelitische Annalen," for Oct., 1840. That Rabbinical Jews actually pray *to* the dead for intercession with God, appears from the following passage of the Talmud (Moed-Taanith, ii. 16, col. 1):—" Why do we go and pray on the graves? There is a difference between R. Levi bar Khanna and R. Hhanina; one says (because it is written), ' Behold, we are counted like the dead before thee.' The other says, ' In order that the dead may seek mercy for us.' What is the reason of this difference? The graves of the Gentiles." Upon this Rashi explains, " Where there are no Jewish graves; for the Gentiles cannot ask mercy for themselves, how much less then for us?"

[2] " Jewish Intelligence," July, 1842.

Being such, in the investigations that may be hereafter made regarding them, it will be of importance to ascertain whether or not those religious customs and regulations in which they differ from the Occidental Jews, are referable to the ordinances of Ezra; and the following points, also, it would be useful to determine:—

Among their books, have they the "Eighteen Blessings," with directions for the attitude during their recital? Have they the chapters of the Fathers? or the Targums, or Zohar? Have they the ancient hymn, which welcomes the Sabbath-day as a bride? And what is the general outline of their liturgical services?

In their expectations do they look for a restoration to Jerusalem? and do they pray, "Bring us to Zion, thy city, with a song; lead us up with joy to our land; lead us securely to our land?" Do they pray, "Make us to rejoice in Elijah the prophet thy servant, and in the dominion of the house of David the Messiah! .... Let not another sit upon his throne, and let not strangers inherit his glory any more?" and if they have not the whole prophecy of Daniel, do they make computations as to the time of Christ's coming, from traditions of the school of Elijah?

As to their relation with Gentiles, do they assign to the latter the seven precepts of Noah? Have they in their Liturgy this thanksgiving? "We laud thee, that thou hast not made us like the nations of the world, nor like the families of the earth; that thou hast not given to us the lot of their assembly; for they bow down to vanity and emptiness, they pray to a god who cannot save." Do they believe that "All Israel has a portion in the world to come?"

In theological doctrine, what is their interpretation of the Old Testament term, "Holy Spirit?" Have they any notion of a mediator between God and man, "the Metatron, the Prince of *thy* countenance?" or of the personal "Word of the Lord," as the Targums have preserved the traditional expressions. Do they retain the idea of Trinity in God's unity, as it is in Zohar? Do they feel the necessity of vicarious sacrifice, as it is written in the Talmud (Moed-Joma, c. 1), "For these things there is

---

[1] לאל לא יושיע. In "Alenu le-shabeahh" of the Sephardim Liturgy.

no atonement but by blood." And do they on the eve of the Day of Atonement sacrifice a cock because its Hebrew name is the same with that of man?

Finally, do they pretend to any traditional decisions upon the law as transmitted from Mount Sinai? Is there in China a Beth-din of persons speaking Hebrew? Have they still any of the Levite or Priestly families? and what are the names most common among them?

Such are questions which should be proposed by future missionaries to that country whenever they meet with professors of the Hebrew religion, since we have already a good reason to believe that they are in possession of the written law and other Scriptures.

The apocryphal books of Maccabees, Judith, and son of Sirach, deserve an inquiry as to their existence in Hebrew, and if they really exist, as to whether these books have the doctrinal and critical blemishes which disfigure our Greek or Latin copies. Also, it is to be remembered, that the class of books in the Beth-el called *Keang-chang*, has not yet been examined, they may be Targums, or rudiments of Mishna.

But it is a matter of far deeper anxiety to learn whether they have in China the book of

Psalms, and any more of the prophetical books than the portions in the Haphtorah. The Lord Jesus and his apostles made frequent appeal to the Psalms and the Prophets as containing a gradually developed light for showing his approach, his character, and his intentions. And all who now desire the spiritual good of Israel must feel a hope that this long-severed colony has every given means of "searching what, or what manner of time the Spirit of Christ did signify, when it testified beforehand the sufferings of Christ, and the glory that should follow."[1]

The Roman Catholic missionaries, true to their mistaken principle, made little or no use of the written Word of God in conversation with these Israelites. They seem to have regarded the people visited as more properly the subjects of critical learning than of conversion to Christianity, like the Gnostics discovered by the Jesuit Ignatius near Bassora, or the Samaritans, whose text of Scripture served to employ the laudable acumen of Scaliger and Ludolf. This supposition may explain the fact, that during the hundred and ten years of their close vicinity to the synagogue in Kae-fung-foo,

[1] 1 Pet. i. 11.

viz., from 1613 to 1723, there is no mention made of any convert from among that congregation.

Certain it is, that Christianity, originally and essentially a Jewish religion, was scarcely presented even under any modification to the descendants of "faithful Abraham" in China. How unlike to the times of the apostles, when in every city the Gospel was *first* preached to the Jews, and the wonder arose, not as now among Gentiles when Jews are believers, but among Jews that the Gentiles should be allowed to partake in the blessings of Christianity!

It is also remarkable, how very little the missionaries did in the way of literature towards promoting Christianity among the Chinese, either Jews or Gentiles.[1] It is to be feared that besides

---

[1] The ground of this complaint is probably not much diminished at the present day, notwithstanding their mission-establishment at Macao. Morrison has stated ("Chinese Miscellany," 1825), "I knew personally ten Catholic missionaries in China, Italians, French, and Portuguese, who had resided at Court, or on the frontier from fourteen to thirty years, and only three of them could read Chinese. Four of these had been many years in Pe-king, and did not know a single Chinese character: they, however, could speak the language, whereas some of the others alluded to could neither read nor speak it."

the supineness just hinted at, their reliance on oral instruction, with crucifixes and pictures, must have left the adherents of the synagogue at liberty to couple or confound their Madonna with the Pagan idols *Teën-how*, the Queen of Heaven; the *Hwüy-füh-foo-jin*, a goddess having a child in her arms; the *Kwan-yin*, the merciful goddess; or even the *Chin-te*, a goddess represented with numerous arms, denoting her varied power to save; while the crucifix would only corroborate such misapprehension, and the sign of the cross become identified with the popular superstition that the numeral which it represents is "the number of perfection."

Trigaut, when narrating the interview of Ricci with one of this people, in the haughty spirit of Romanism, only relates the event as a proof that "Jewish filth" was found even there;[1] and Semmedo, afterwards describing the neatness of the synagogue, digresses with the ill-natured remark, "If any synagogue is free from uncleanness"[2]—the very taunt of the ancient Pharisees against the Gentiles, as the "common or unclean." True, indeed, that sin-

[1] "Judæam etiam fæcem in hæc regna confluxisse deprendimus." (De Christianâ expeditione, &c.)
[2] "Si limpia ay sinagoga." (Imperio, &c.)

fulness without the means of pardon is spiritual leprosy without hope, but a right-minded Christian will remember " who has made him to differ," who it was that said to him individually, "I will, be thou clean!" and thus be very humble: but when the Roman Church cherishes an unkindly feeling towards the fallen Jews, the Apostle Paul has provided a rebuke in his caution given expressly to that particular Church: " Be not highminded, but fear: for if God spared not the natural branches, take heed lest also he spare not thee. Behold therefore the goodness and severity of God: on them which fell, severity; but toward thee, goodness, if thou continue in his goodness: otherwise thou also shalt be cut off."[1] Thus declaring with authority that Rome is no more infallible than Jerusalem.

In reviewing the past ages of Israelitish sojourn in China, as well as our limited knowledge will permit, we immediately feel how happily tame is that retrospect compared with the dark and sanguinary annals of Jews in Mohammedan and Popish realms, for the toleration of the Chinese spirit has never yet discovered that the Hebrew passover is cele-

[1] Rom. xi. 21, 22.

brated with an appetite for human blood; and happy is the nation which, while it has had an opportunity to do so, has not persecuted them for religion's sake, because it is written, "I will bless them that bless thee, and curse him that curseth thee."[1]

The Jews must have been contented settlers at the extreme east, living principally in accordance with the genius of Mosaic institutions and Chinese predilections, as agriculturists in the delicious climate of that "flowery land." Still, if one prediction of the Bible be as true as another, there must have been vicissitudes in their history; and though it is not clear as to what extent they may have been exempt from "the trembling heart and sorrow of mind," denounced in Deuteronomy, and known to be the general inheritance of their kindred in other lands, yet they certainly do seem to be a timorous and a suspicious people.

Israel in China has resembled some plant endued with a wonderful force of vegetation, a force not to be implied from its vast increase of production, not shown by a power of overcoming obstacles, but rather by an inherent faculty of protracting a lingering existence. Our

[1] Gen. xii. 3.

information about them has dwindled to a mere point: still it may be trusted in a Christian spirit that this probable decay is not in truth a process of extinction; that if synagogues yet remain in the western provinces of Sze-chuen and Shen-se, they may be speedily discovered, and that the Church of God may even yet have the pleasure to behold them disseminating a saving knowledge among the Heathen.

The Talmud says,[1] that "the Lord could not find a vessel to contain a larger blessing for his people Israel than peace." Some pious persons have attributed the general quietude of Chinese history, with prolonged enjoyment of their peculiar institutions (and certainly in this condition their Hebrew guests are to be included, and for the same reason), to the blessing resting on the paternal spirit which pervades the latter. The basis of civil obedience being laid in filial reverence, "Honour thy father and thy mother, that thy days may be long in the land which the Lord thy God giveth thee," is a conditional benediction which remains valid till parental relations shall be no more, and applicable to national as well as individual prosperity. The Chinese teachers are unanimous in the

[1] Mishnah (Taharoth, Oketsim).

inculcation of this principle in their political philosophy. " Duty to parents is that by which we should serve a prince. . . . . When families are virtuous the nation will grow up virtuous. . . . . . In order to that which is called governing a nation, there must be the regulation of families. Not to be capable of teaching a family, and yet to be able to teach a nation of men, there is no such thing."[1] What precious elements are combined in this patriarchal wisdom! Surely this is the conservative influence which has crystallized the virtues and the peace of that vast empire for untold generations. It is true that errors have been perpetuated by the same principle; but to this we also look forward in expectation of Christianity being hereafter embraced there by whole families and cities at a time.

The Hebrew Scriptures have too long remained unfruitful in China, where the traditions and maxims of the people do not lead to everlasting happiness. It is now time that our whole revelation of God be sent freely forth in that widely-spread language; and that

[1] Ta-hio, in " Morrison's View," &c.

the Israelites, no longer reading the law through a veil,[1] but being taught the truth of Messiah, should begin to fulfil in reality their own destiny to be " a kingdom of priests."

Then when the aspiration of St. Paul within the Mamertine prison in Rome is accomplished, as he exclaimed, " But the Word of God is not bound!"—when his generous call is loudly answered, " Rejoice, ye Gentiles, with his people!"—then, in China, as in every other empire, man, universal man, shall delight to heap up the choicest treasures of external wealth, of genius, of intellect, and self-sacrifice, in honour of that loveliest character, that holiest Being, who came into this world to be, in combination with his other benevolent offices, " a light to lighten the Gentiles, and the glory of his people Israel!"

[1] 2 Cor. iii. 13—17.

# APPENDIX.

### A. (*Page* 25.)

שמע ישראל יהוה אלהינו יהוה אחד
ברוך שם כבוד מלכותו לעלם ועד :

### B. (*Page* 25)

ב׳כ׳ב׳ יהוה אלהי האלהים ואדוני
האל הגדול הגבור והנורא :

Tychsen understands by ב׳כ׳ב׳, the phrase
ברוך יהוה כל יום כי :

### C. (*Page* 42)

THE following is a sketch of the method of calculation :—

The Jews did not compute by the *æra of creation* till after the completion of the Talmud ; and they confess it was not generally adopted till after the death of R. Sherira, A.D. 1019. Before that time they used the *æra of contracts*, which æra dates from some year (the year is disputed) of the reign of Alexander the Great; and is, therefore, the same with the Gentile æra of the Seleucides, or Alexander. It is employed in Josephus and in the Maccabees.

According to Bartoloccio (Bibl. Rabb., t. 2, p. 430, et seq.), all Jewish authors make the *æra of contracts* to begin in the year 1000, from the departure out of Egypt, i.e., in the year of the world 3448, and 312 before the Christian æra. But the years of this *æra of contracts* being civil years, commenced in the month Nisan (March—April); the difference, therefore, between that and the Christian æra is 312 years and about ten months.

It is universally acknowledged that the Jews entered China before the adoption of the *æra of creation;* they therefore use the *æra of contracts,* and their year 1933 in the manuscript corresponds with A.D. 1621.

But the month Ab, or fifth moon of 1933, answers to the twelfth moon of the year of the world 5380, which was an embolismic year, and so becomes July—August of A.D. 1620.

Likewise the month Iyar of 1937, is shown to correspond with April—May of A.D. 1624.

The separate particulars of this computation being all verified with severe exactness, the matter seems to be finally decided. It is republished, and therefore with approval, by O. G. Tychsen, in

"Abhandlung von der Jahrzahlen der Juden."— (P. 9.)

---

### D. (*Page* 42)

The following is the original, from the " Notitiæ, &c.," of Kœgler:—

דר במדינת באול בין ליגנן שהר כודאי אזמד אסמאן תורה פוגאה שה פרשה המה ישראל סוחון מאן ניושת אול תורה צולי אלף תשעה מאה שלשים שלש מאהי אב הדא בשבא שלש רוזי ּ ניושת תורה תאטן צלי אלף תשעה מאה שלשים שבע מאהי אייר ערבעה בשבא עשר שני רוזי ּ מרינו רבינו רבי יעקוב בן רבי אבישי בן רבי אלדד הספר המלמד השליחי : השליה רבי שאדי בן רבי יעקוב ּ ניושאו צלו רבי מורדכי בן שמעון בנישת רבי עקיבה בר אהרן בן עזרא נדר נדבח הבחור שמחה בר יהשוי בן יוסף ּ גואה רבי יעקוב בר ראובן בן בוזי ּ מורדכי בר בנימין בוז בוי ּ ברוך אתה בבאך וברוך אתה בצאתך ּ כבד מאד במקניה בכסף לישועתך קויתי יהוה :

---

### E. (*Pages* 46, 67.)

The learned Abel-Remusat has written a "Memoir on the Opinions of Lao-tseu, a Chinese

Philosopher of the Sixth Century before our Æra, who professed the opinions commonly attributed to Pythagoras, Plato, and their Disciples." (Paris, 1823.) One passage quoted is most interesting, as exhibiting the gleams of light in ancient traditions, both with respect to the ineffable name, and the doctrine of the Trinity :—

"That for which you look, and which you see not, is called I; that towards which you listen, yet hear not, is called Hi (the letter H); what your hand seeks, and yet feels not, is called Wei (the letter V). These three are inscrutable, and being united form only one. Of them the superior is not more bright, nor the inferior more obscure. . . . . . . This is what is called form without form, image without image, an indefinable Being! Precede it, and ye find not its beginning; follow it, and ye discover not its end."

Upon this Dr. Wiseman writes in his " Twelve Lectures on the Connexion between Science and Revealed Religion,"—" I need only remark, with Abel-Remusat, that the extraordinary name given to this triune essence, is composed of the three letters, I. H. V., for the syllables expressed in the Chinese have no meaning in that language, and are consequently representative of the mere letters. It is, therefore, a foreign name, and we shall seek for it in vain anywhere but among the Jews. Their ineffable name, as it was called, which we pronounce Jehovah, is to be met variously distorted in the mysteries of many Heathen nations, but in none less disfigured than in this passage of a Chinese phi-

losopher. Indeed, it could not have been possibly expressed in his language in any manner more closely approaching the original. . . . . . .
Ιαω is probably the Greek form approaching nearest to the true pronunciation of the Hebrew name. Even pronouncing the Chinese word according to its syllables, *I-hi-wei*, we have a nearer approach to the Hebrew, *Je-ho-wa*, as the Oriental Jews rightly pronounce it, than in the Chinese word, *Chi-li-see-tu-see*, to its original, *Christus*."— (Lecture xi.)

F. (*Page 52*)

מטטרון : סנדלפון : ענאל׳ : רפאל׳ : מיכאל׳ : גבריאל׳ : אוריאל׳ : בריאל׳ : צדקיאל׳ : צופיאל׳ : ידידיאל׳

מיכאל׳

גבריאל׳

רפאל׳

# CHINESE JEWS

A LECTURE
delivered by

MARCUS N. ADLER, M.A.

*at*

THE JEWS' COLLEGE LITERARY SOCIETY
Queen Square House, London
on June 17, 1900

## CHINESE JEWS.

THE Chinese and the Jews belong to the oldest nations in the world, but whilst the Chinese are the most isolated and self-contained of peoples, it may be said of the Jews that they are the most wide-spread and scattered. I propose to give the result of some inquiries into the question of how the Jews have fared in the Celestial Empire.

It is only in quite recent times that any Jewish writer has so much as noticed the existence of a Jewish settlement in China. Benjamin of Tudela refers to the country, but, well informed as he was, he makes no mention of the existence of a Jewish colony there.

We owe to the Jesuits the first authenticated accounts we possess [1]. It was in the time of Queen Elizabeth that the Church of Rome sent out to China a band of missionaries who happened to be men of the world, and withal, men of culture and knowledge. They were well received in Pekin. Several of them were even raised to the rank of Mandarin. As Presidents of the Tribunal of Mathematics they advised the Government as to the Calendar, and assisted the Astronomical Board. Father Ricci was one of the first of these missionaries, and in the report to the Propaganda Fide, at Rome, we are told how he came to know about the existence of Chinese Jews.

One summer day, in the early part of the seventeenth century, Ricci received a visit from a scholar who had come to Pekin in order to pass his examination for a government appointment. The candidate was anxious to make the acquaintance of one who, he surmised, must be

[1] Trigaltius, *de Christiano Expeditione apud Sinas*, Aug.Vind., 1615. A. Semmedo, *Letters from Jesuit Missions*, 1627. Id., *Further Reports*, Madrid, 1642.

a co-religionist, for it was said that he worshipped one God, the Lord of heaven and earth, and yet was not a Mohammedan. Father Ricci was struck with his visitor's features, so different from those of an ordinary Chinaman, and took him to his cratory, where he knelt before the picture of the Holy Family with St. John the Baptist, and another, that of the Evangelists. The visitor did so likewise, saying, "We in China do reverence to our ancestors. This is Rebecca with her sons Jacob and Esau, but as to the other picture, why make obeisance to only four sons of Jacob, were there not twelve?" Then mutual explanations were given. The visitor was an Israelite, Ngai by name, who had come to Pekin from Kai-fung-foo, the ancient capital of Ho-nan. In this city, the visitor explained, his community had a synagogue which they had recently repaired, and in which there was a roll of the Law which was over 400 years old. "At Hang-chow-foo," he said, "there was a larger congregation of Jews, who also had a synagogue; Jews dwelt in other provinces also."

Father Ricci was able to verify all these statements, and received visits from other native Jews. Julius Aleni, his successor, had a fair knowledge of Hebrew, and he paid the congregation a visit in 1613. Semmedo, writing in 1642, reports that Jews were living in four Chinese towns, and that they were much respected.

At the beginning of the eighteenth century we have further accounts from the Jesuits. Gozani, one of them, wrote a letter from Kai-fung-foo, dated November 5, 1704, giving full details of the Jewish customs, and describing their synagogue. Later on Domengo sketched a plan of the communal buildings, and Fathers Gaubil and Cibot obtained copies and translations of the inscriptions on the walls and on certain monumental stones [1].

[1] *Lettres édifiantes et curieuses, écrites des Missions étrangères par quelques Missionaires de la Compagnie de Jésus.* Paris, vol. VII, 1707. Id., *Reports of Gaubil and Domengo*, vol. XXXI, 1774. *Commentatio de Iudaeis Sinensibus*, an Appendix to Brotier's *Tacitus*. Paris, 1771.

Quite recently Père Tobar has published, under the auspices of the Roman Catholic Mission at Shanghai, a most valuable work [1] on these inscriptions. Facsimiles and translations into French of the inscriptions on the stone tablets or steles severally dated 1489, 1512, and 1663, are given along with twenty-three horizontal and seventeen vertical inscriptions which were found in the synagogue. We must indeed be thankful to the Jesuits for having placed within our reach these precious records of the past. The following are abstracts of the dated inscriptions:—

## I. Abstract of Inscription on Stone Stele of 1489.

Abraham was the nineteenth in descent from Adam.

The patriarchs handed down the tradition forbidding the making and worshipping of images and spirits, and the holding of superstitions.

Abraham pondered over problems of Nature and arrived at the belief in the one true God and became the founder of the religion we believe in to this day. This happened in the 146th year of the Tcheou dynasty.

His belief was handed down from father to son till Moses, who, it is found, was alive in the 613th year of the Tcheou dynasty. He was endowed with wisdom and virtue. He abode forty days on the summit of Mount Sinai, refraining from meat and drink, and communing with God. The fifty-three portions of the Law had their origin with him. From him the Law and tradition was handed down unto Ezra, who was likewise a patriarch.

Man in his daily pursuits must ever have God before him. We pray three times a day: morning, noon, and evening.

When praying, the worshipper first bends his body; then in silent devotion he offers up his prayer or raises his voice, swaying, meanwhile, to and fro. At the end, he retires three paces and advances five, then turns towards the left and right, and finally looks upwards and downwards, to show his belief that God is everywhere.

It is incumbent upon the Jew to venerate his ancestors. Twice in the year, in the spring and in the autumn, he offers them oxen and sheep together with the fruits of the season.

---

[1] *Inscriptions Juives de K'ai-fong-fou*, par le P. Jérôme Tobar, S.J. *Variétés Sinologiques*, No. 17, Chang-hai, 1900.

Four days every month are devoted to purification and to stimulating to charitable acts. Each seventh day is devoted to rest, and a fresh period of good deeds then commences anew. In the fourth season of the year, the Jew places himself under severe restraint for seven days. One entire day he abstains altogether from food, devoting it to prayer and repentance.

Our religion came originally from Tien-tchou (India ?).

Seventy families, viz. Li, Yen, Kao, Tchao, and others, came to the Court of Song, bringing as tribute cloth of cotton from Western lands. The emperor said, "You have come to China. Keep and follow the customs of your forefathers, and settle at Peën-lang (Kai-fung-foo)."

In the first year of Long-hing of the Song dynasty (1163), when Lie-wei (Levi) was the Ouseta (Rabbi), Yentula erected the synagogue. Under the Yuen dynasty, in the sixteenth year of the Tche-yuen cycle (1279) the temple structures were rebuilt. The dimensions on each side were thirty-five tchang (about 350 feet).

The Emperor Tai-tsou, who founded the Ming dynasty, granted in 1390 land to all who submitted to his authority, on which they could dwell peacefully and profess their religion without molestation. The Jews had ministers of religion who were called Man-la (Mullah) to rule the synagogue and to watch over the religious institutions.

In the nineteenth year of Yong-lo (1421), Yen-Tcheng, a physician, received from the emperor a present of incense and permission to repair the synagogue. Then was received the grand tablet of the Ming dynasty to be placed in the synagogue. The emperor bestowed honours and titles upon Yen-Tcheng.

In 1461 there was an overflow of the Yellow River, and the foundations alone of the structure were left standing. Li-yong, having obtained the necessary permission from the provincial treasurer, rebuilt the temple and had it decorated.

Later on, the cells at the rear of the synagogue were put up, and three copies of the Holy Law were placed there. A copy of the Law had before this been obtained from Ning-pouo; another had been presented by Tchao-Yng of Ning-pouo. Various dignitaries presented the table of offerings, the bronze vase, the flower vases, and the candlesticks. Other members of the community contributed the ark, the triumphal arch, the balustrades, and other furniture for Israel's temple called I-se-lo-nie-tien.

All this has been recorded, to be handed down to the latest generations by me, Kin-Tchong, literary graduate, and engraved by others on durable stone on this stele in the second year of Hong-Tche (1489).

## II. Inscription on Stone Stele of 1512.

Erected by Tsouo Tang, a mandarin, and other dignitaries in the seventh year of Tcheng-te of the Ming dynasty, when a copy of the Law was presented by Kin-Pou of Wei-yang. The inscription gives details of the Jewish religion, its moral and other ordinances, and its canonical books, together with the historical incidents already referred to in Inscription I. The following passage is of interest :—"After the Creation, the Doctrine was transmitted by Adam to Noah; thence unto Abraham, Isaac, and Jacob, and afterwards through the twelve patriarchs to Moses, Aaron, and Joshua. Ezra promulgated the Law, and through him the letters of the Yew-thae (Jewish) nation were made plain."

## III. Inscription on Stone Stele of 1663.

In a long preamble an attempt is made to show that there is nothing in the Sacred Law of the Jews which is not in conformity with the six canonical books of the Chinese. Then follow notices of the Jewish settlement and of the historical incidents already referred to in Inscription I. A graphic account is given of the events which followed the fall of the Ming dynasty in 1642. The city of Kaifung-foo, then called Peën-lang, stood six-months' siege by the rebel chief Li Tse-tcheng, who eventually caused the fall of the city by diverting the Yellow River. The loss of life was great, and the synagogue was destroyed; 200 and odd Jewish families were saved, and took refuge on the north side of the river. The names are recorded of those who succeeded in saving the scrolls and other sacred books which were floating on the water. These, with other sacred writings which were rescued out of the ruins of the synagogue, were placed in a large house away from the city, where, for a time, the Jews assembled for divine service. About ten years afterwards, Tchao Yng-tcheng, a Jewish mandarin from the province of Chen-si, who was in command of a force of soldiers, came to Peën and did much to restore the city, the roads and the bridges. Aided by his brother, Yng-teou, he induced his co-religionists to return to the city and to take up their old habitations close to the temple which was rebuilt in the year 1653, in the tenth year of the reign of Choen-tche. Full particulars are given of the work of reconstruction and of the part taken by the members of the seven houses. It was not possible to make up more than one complete scroll of the Law out of the parchments recovered from the waters. This task was entrusted to their religious chief. The scroll, much venerated by the faithful, was placed in the middle of the ark. Twelve other scrolls were gradually collated and put in order by members of the community, whose several names are given on the back of the stele, and the other holy writings and prayer-books were repaired and revised with every care. The commandant Tchao Yng-tcheng, before leaving the city, wrote an account of the vicissitudes undergone by the sacred scrolls, and his brother published a book of ten chapters on the subject. Several high mandarins, whose names are given in the stele, took a part in the work of the restoration of the synagogue, also in the erection of the stele, which took place in the second year of Kang-hi of the Tsing dynasty (1663).

Summarizing the historical references in these inscriptions, and in the accounts of the Jesuit fathers and other reliable writers [1], we arrive at the following results:— Jews had certainly settled in China some time during the Han dynasty, which ruled from 200 B.C. to 220 A.C. It is supposed that the settlement took place soon after the year 34 A.C., at which time terrible persecutions of the Jews took place in Babylon; no less than 50,000 were then massacred. Others hold that the settlement took place thirty-five years later, after the fall of Jerusalem. It is quite possible that the Jewish colony in China may be of even older date. Having regard to the fact that the trade route of ancient times from China and India was not exclusively maritime, but crossed the steppes and highlands of Central Asia, and then passed through Media, Mesopotamia and Syria, it is not at all impossible that sections of the ten tribes of Israel may have found their way to China, as we believe they did find their way to Cochin China. A passage in 2 Kings xvii. 6 is to the effect that Shalmaneser carried Israel away and placed them in Halah and in Habor by the river of Gozan, and in the cities of the Medes.

[1] C. G. von Murr, *Versuch einer Geschichte der Juden in Sina*; nebst P. Ignaz Koeglers Beschreibung ihrer heiligen Bücher. Halle, 1806. *Jewish Expositor*, vol. I. London, 1815. E. C. Bridgman, *The Chinese Repository*. Canton, 1834. Terrien de Lacouperie, *Babylonian and Oriental Record*. London, 1886, &c. Henri Cordier, *Les Juifs en Chine*. Paris, 1891. Rev. A. Kingsley Glover, *Jewish Chinese Papers*, 1894. Alexander Wylie, *Chinese Researches*, Shanghai, 1897.

The allusion in Isa. xlix. 12, "Behold, these shall come from far: and, lo, these from the north and the west; and these from the land of Sinim," points to China.

In Renaudot's translation of "Ancient accounts of India and China, by two Mohammedan travellers who went there in the ninth century [1]," we read that over 100,000 Mohammedans, Jews, Parsees, and Christians, who came to China for purposes of commerce, perished in the Bai-chu revolts. From incidental remarks in Marco Polo's *Travels*, we learn that the Jews were sufficiently numerous in his time (1286) to exercise political influence in China and Tartary.

Ibn Batuta, a writer of the fourteenth century, states that Jews then resided in China [2]. In his account of the city of Khansa (Hangchow), he remarks: "In the second division are the Jews, Christians, and the Turks; these are numerous, and their number is not known, and theirs is the most beautiful city. Their streets are well disposed, and their great men are wealthy."

In those days Kai-fung-foo, called by the Tartars Peënlang, was a city six leagues in circumference; Gibbon states that over one million families dwelt in it. Naturally the Jews would flock to such a city for trading purposes, and so we find that in the days of the Emperor Heao-tsong many Jews came thither by way of Persia and Khorassan. They won the emperor's favour by presents of cotton or cloth.

In course of time the city suffered from inundations of the Yellow River, and frequent conflagrations sadly reduced its importance. The Jewish quarter was not more than five hundred feet from the river embankment, and was specially prone to damage by floods. In 1642 the city was besieged; the embankments were demolished, 100,000 people perished, and many Hebrew manuscripts were destroyed. We read of

---

[1] Translated from the Arabic by E. Renaudot. Paris, 1718.
[2] *The Travels of Ibn Batuta.* Translated from the Arabic by Rev. Dr. Lee. Issued by London Oriental Translation Fund, 1829.

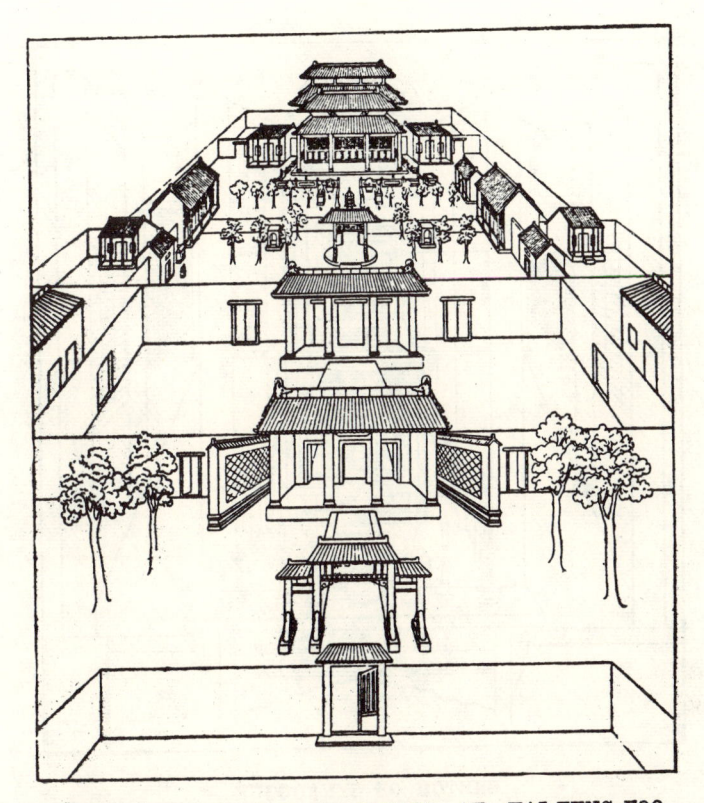

SKETCH OF TEMPLE BUILDINGS AT KAI-FUNG-FOO.
(*From designs of* FATHERS DOMENGO *and* BRUCKER.)

Entrance.
Pai-leou or Triumphal Arch.
Grand Portal with side entrances.
Portico with side entrances.
Triumphal Arch.
Stone Steles.
Façade of Temple.
Space for erection of Tabernacle on Festival.
Two Lions on Pedestals.
Vessel for Incense.
Flower Vases.
Halls for Assembly.
Site for the Extraction of Nerves and Sinews.
Hall of Ancestors.
Tchao's Reception Room.
Another Reception Room.
Dwelling-Houses for Caretakers.

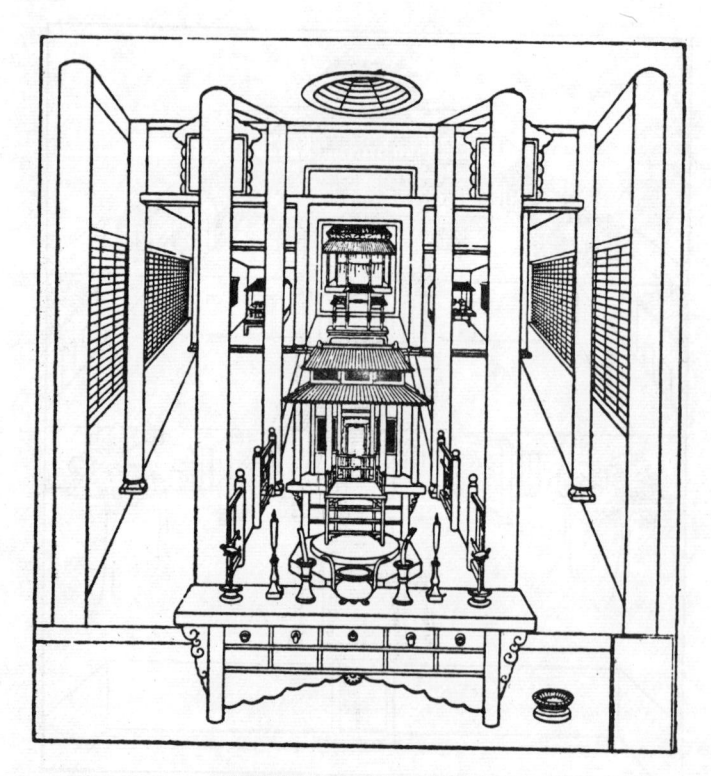

**SKETCH OF SYNAGOGUE.**

Large Table for Incense.
Chair of Moses or Pulpit.
Balustrade reaching to the Bethel.
Tablet with Prayer for Emperor.
Arcade with Inscription.
Beth 1 surmounted with a Dome.
Cells for Scrolls.
Columns.
Windows.
Repositories for Prayer Books and Bibles.
Basin for Washing of Hands.
Two Tablets on which the Ten Commandments were emblazoned.
Inscription, "Hear, O Israel."
Dome surmounting Chair of Moses.

the synagogue being rebuilt 1279, and again in 1489, and of its restoration at the commencement of the seventeenth century, and again in 1653.

Thanks to the explicit accounts of the Jesuits, we are in a position to give a very full description of the communal buildings as they appeared in the early and middle part of the eighteenth century, and these accounts tally with those of the Protestant Mission in 1850, and of recent visitors, who, however, only saw the ruins of what must have been a noble cluster of buildings.

The site covered a space of from three to four hundred feet by 150 feet, and there were four courts proceeding from east to west. The synagogue proper faced west, the direction in which Jerusalem lay. In the centre of the first court there stood a large triumphal arch, called Paileou, adorned with a Chinese inscription recording its dedication to the Creator and Preserver of all. There were bath-houses and water-chambers in the precincts of this court. The second court was entered by a great gate (only opened on great occasions), and by side doors. The walls were flanked north and south by dwelling-houses for caretakers and keepers. The third court had in its centre a small triumphal arch, flanked on each side by pavilions in which were enshrined two of the engraved stone tablets of which I have already given an account. On the south side of this court was a commemorative chapel in memory of a Jewish mandarin, Tchao, a mandarin of the second degree, who rebuilt the synagogue after its destruction by fire. And on the north side there was another chapel in memory of one who erected the edifice then standing. There were also reception-rooms for guests. The fourth court was divided by a long avenue of trees. Halfway stood a great brazen vase of incense, on each side of which there was a brazen vase containing flowers, and a marble lion upon a pedestal. Adjoining the northern wall was a recess in which the nerves and sinews of the animals slain for food were extracted. Some importance seems to have been attached to this rite, and up to the present time the Jewish community are known under the name of "Teaou-kin-keaou," the sect "that pluck out the sinews." In the second division of the court was the hall of ancestors (Tsoo-tang). Here were venerated—probably at the high festivals in the spring and autumn—the Patriarchs of Old Testament history after the Chinese manner. The name of each was recorded on a tablet; there were no pictures; to each of them was assigned a censer for incense, the largest being for Abraham, others for the other patriarchs, Moses, Aaron, Joshua and Ezra. Then there was an open place where they put up every year, on the Feast of Tabernacles, a booth covered with boughs and ornamented with flowers.

The synagogue proper was a building sixty feet by forty feet, to which access was gained by a portico with a double row of four columns. The handsome roof was supported by columns in the usual style of Chinese domestic architecture.

In the centre of the building was the so-called chair of Moses[1], corresponding, I presume, to our platform, the Almemar; it was a grand seat or pulpit with an embroidered cushion, on which the scrolls of the Law were laid when opened for reading. In front of this pulpit was a tablet on which the name of the emperor was emblazoned in golden letters with a prayer that he might live ten thousand myriads of years. From the dome above were suspended the words in Hebrew—"Hear, O Israel, the Lord our God! The Lord is one!" and other appropriate quotations in Hebrew. On a large table by the door stood six candelabra, a vase for incense, and a tablet recording the acts of kindness of the emperors of the Ming dynasty, who had directed the burning of the incense.

At the western extremity of the building, on an elevation,

---

[1] See correspondence in *Revue des Études Juives*, vol. XXXV, p. 110. The Hon. Mayer Sulzberger calls attention to Matt. xxiii. 2.

was the so-called Teën-lang—the House of Heaven—or Bethel, as the Jesuits call it, to which access was gained by steps on both sides. Here the ministering Rabbi and priests only were allowed to enter. In the Teën-lang were placed the thirteen scrolls of the Law, each in a separate case, and enclosed in silk curtains. The scroll in the middle was the one most venerated, and it would appear

CHAIR OF MOSES.

that the other ten or all the twelve were merely copies or transcribed from the venerated one in the middle. At the western end of the building two tablets were conspicuous; they were inscribed with the Ten Commandments in golden letters. The synagogue was known in Chinese as the "Li-pai-se," meaning the weekly meeting-house, because the principal meeting was held on the Sabbath Day.

Father Domengo describes fully the visit he paid to the synagogue on Saturday, October 3, 1722. It happened that this was the eighth day of the festival of Tabernacles, and the visitor comments upon the fact that the portion of the Law that was read upon that day was not the festival portion, but the Song of Moses, Deut. xxxi–xxxii. The following day was the Rejoicing of the Law; which the congregants celebrated, as we do, by making circuits with the scrolls around the synagogue.

As in most Eastern countries, worshippers used to take off their shoes when they entered the house of God, and they put on a blue head-dress in contradistinction to the Mohammedans in China, who used a white head-dress. Whilst reciting the Law the reader covered his face with a transparent veil of gauze, and wore a red silk scarf dependent from the right shoulder and tied under the left arm; by his side stood a monitor to correct him if necessary. The Hebrew books were kept in repositories at the synagogue, and they were rarely allowed to be taken home. This may account for the ignorance of their literature shown by the Chinese Jews. The missionaries give full information as to the mode in which the Jews pronounced the Hebrew. The calendar and the mode in which the festivals were fixed were identical with our own, and resemble in many respects the calendar of the Chinese themselves, who, like the Jews, regulate the year by the moon, the ordinary year consisting of twelve lunar months, every second or third year being a leap year consisting of thirteen months. The Sabbath they observed with great strictness; the food was prepared on the day preceding. Their customs and observances accorded entirely with those of the Rabbinitic Jews of the present day with the one exception that they regarded the New Moon as a festival.

In 1723 the efforts of the missionaries were put a stop to by the Chinese Government.

It was only gradually that the fact of the existence of

a Jewish colony in China came to the knowledge of the Jews in Europe. I found among the MSS. in the British Museum an elaborate letter written in elegant Hebrew by the Haham Isaac, the son of the well-known David Nieto, dated Adar 1, 5520, that is the year 1760[1], in which, in the name of the London Jewish Community, he affectionately addressed his brethren dwelling in the furthermost East, and implores them to tell him as to their condition and their origin. He subjoins a list of questions which he asks them to answer. Appended to this document is a letter, unsigned, addressed by the writer at the request of his friend, Mr. David Salamons, to a member of the East India Company, asking him for his good offices in getting the letter delivered to the Jewish community in China.

My brother, Elkan Adler, has called my attention to a book written originally in Hebrew by a Morocco Rabbi—Moses Edrehi by name—which was translated into English and published in 1836. Nieto's letter is given in full, and Edrehi states " an answer to the letter was received, and it was couched in the Chinese and Hebrew languages." The original was placed in the museum at the India House. Edrehi says he could not find it. I regret to say I have had no better success.

In the year 1815 some English Jews sent a letter by way of Canton, and a travelling bookseller is reported to have delivered it. But no reply was received.

In 1842 the Treaty of Nankin was concluded, under which five treaty ports were opened to commerce. It was at that time that Mr. James Finn, who subsequently became British Consul at Jerusalem, began to interest himself in the Chinese Jews[2]. In a little book entitled *The Orphan Colony of Jews in China* published in 1872, he gives the text of a letter composed both in Chinese and Hebrew,

---
[1] B. M. additional MSS. 29868.
[2] James Finn, *The Jews in China*. London, 1843. Id., *The Orphan Colony of Jews in China*. London, 1872.

of which the British Consul at Amoy took charge. This reached the hands of the Jews, and the reply, which Mr. Finn did not receive till the year 1870, was very pathetic. The colony seems to have been rapidly declining, their teachers had all died, and there was no one left who could read Hebrew. "Daily with tears in our eyes we call on the Holy Name; if we could but again procure ministers and put our house of prayer in order, our religion would have a firm support."

In the year 1850 a Bishopric was established at Hongkong, and it was in consequence of a visit which the Rt. Rev. Dr. Smith, Bishop of Victoria, paid to Shanghai, where the London Missionary Society had a branch, that it was decided to send some missionaries to inquire as to the condition of the Jews at Kai-fung-foo. Two Chinese Christians were selected, and, with a view to obtain a ready hearing from the Jews, letters of introduction, drawn up in Hebrew, were obtained from some Jewish Bagdad merchants at Shanghai. The messengers started from Shanghai on November 15, 1850, and travelled by way of the Grand Canal and the Yellow River. I will quote the very words of the Bishop[1]. "Here in the midst of the surrounding population, two-thirds of whom were Mohammedans, close to a heathen temple dedicated to the god of fire, were found a few Jewish families, sunk in the lowest poverty and destitution—their religion scarcely more than a name, and yet sufficient to separate them from the multitude around. Exposed to trial, reproach, and the pain of long-deferred hope, they remained the anxious repositories of the Oracle of God, and survived as the solitary witnesses of departed glory. Not one could read Hebrew— their Rabbi had died fifty years ago; the synagogue tottering in ruins, they had petitioned the Chinese Emperor to have pity on their poverty and to rebuild their temple. No reply had been received from Pekin, but to this feeble hope

[1] *The Jews at Kae-fung-foo*, London Missionary Society's Press. Shang-hae, 1851. *Jewish Intelligence.* London, 1853, &c.

they still clung. Out of seventy clans only seven remained, numbering about 200 persons. A few were shopkeepers in the city, others were agriculturists on land a little distance from the suburbs, whilst a few lived in the temple precincts almost destitute of raiment and shelter."

The Jews had no hesitation in trusting the messengers, for in comparing the Hebrew writing of the letter of introduction with their own Holy Writings they saw that the style of writing was similar. The men left after a short stay, taking with them eight small books, containing each one of the Sabbath sections of the Law in Hebrew, facsimiles of which have been published.

A few months later the envoys came again, provided this time with some hundreds of pounds, part of the proceeds of a legacy left by Miss Cook to the Missionary Society. This time they secured six copy scrolls, thirty of the weekly portions of the Law, and over thirty quarto books on Chinese paper, containing in more or less complete form the prayers for everyday use, and for Sabbaths and festivals. Dr. Neubauer of Oxford has given a full description of these in the eighth volume of the JEWISH QUARTERLY REVIEW [1], an article which Mr. Elkan Adler supplemented in 1898 [2]. They are deposited at the museum at Lincoln's Inn of the London Society for Promoting Christianity among the Jews.

One point is quite clear, that the ritual used by the Chinese Jews is identical with that laid down by Maimonides in the Yad-hachazaka, which is also followed by the Yemen Jews. The Jewish colony may have followed a different ritual in olden times, but the ritual we find established during the last 300 years clearly came by way of Persia; all the rubrics, as Dr. Neubauer has clearly put it, are in the modern Persian language; and the few hymns and poetical additions in the Prayerbook are the same as are found in the old Persian MS. rituals which my brother, Elkan Adler, lately brought

---

[1] J. Q. R., VIII, 123.   [2] J. Q. R., X, 584.

over from Persia and Bokhara. The Jesuit Fathers stated that the Chinese Jews had most of the twenty-four books of the Old Testament more or less complete. No part of the Scriptures beyond the Pentateuch has found its way to Europe. It was stated also that the Jews were in possession of some commentaries called by them Kiangtschang, also of the first and second Books of the Maccabees. The Jesuits tried in vain to obtain a sight of these. To many it will be a surprise to hear that a Hebrew-Syriac version of the second Book of Maccabees existed.

I have examined the scrolls of the Law in possession of the Society, also the scroll presented by the Society to the British Museum. I might add that both the Universities of Oxford and Cambridge have been presented with similar copies. One copy was retained at Hongkong. Dr. Martin has supplied Yale College and the Lennox Library at New York each with a scroll. The Hon. Mayer Sulzberger possesses another [1]. Dr. Scherzer of the Novara Mission obtained a Roll for the Vienna Library, and we learn that quite recently a Roll has been sent on to Paris. In my opinion they are all executed by ignorant scribes. In fact they are "Chinese" copies of the faulty old copy which was so much venerated by the Jews at Kai-fung-foo, under circumstances referred to in the inscription on Tablet III.

It is strange that most of the scrolls and fragments which have come under my view have the first letter of each column commencing with the letter ו vau. This was a practice of comparatively recent introduction. Not all the instructions of the Sopherim have been complied with, but this seems to arise merely from the ignorance or neglect of the scribes who did the work. There are no

[1] My friend writes to me as follows: "If I should live long enough to see the Chinese troubles settled, and a new Synagogue dedicated at Kai-fung-foo, it would give me great pleasure to contribute the roll for the edification of the descendants and successors of the original owners."

תגין Tagin, no majuscular or minuscular letters. The סתומות and פתוחות are done in haphazard fashion. The four blank lines between each of the books are not attended to. In one instance they are found between ויקרא and צו instead of heading ויקרא[1].

The names of the scribes of the weekly portions of the Law in quarto books on Chinese paper are given in several cases. One of these, at the end of the portion of Genesis, writes as follows:—" In the city originally called Peën-lang, the Holy City by the help of Heaven, the Law with its sections was copied in this year 1935; in the month of Ab, the first day of the week and the third day of the month, the writing of the Law, the entire Law, was finished in the year 1937; in the month of Iyar, the fourth day of the week, the twelfth day of the month, our teacher and master Rabbi Jacob, the son of Rabbi Abishai, grandson of Rabbi Eldad, the Scribe and Teacher, completed it," &c. It should be mentioned that the years here quoted are years of the Seleucid era, and 1935 is equivalent, according to our common reckoning, to 1623.

I have already pronounced my opinion that there is nothing to show that the ancient congregations in China were not descended from the ten lost tribes. But no remains of an archaic literature, such as they should have possessed, have as yet been found.

The reports as to the discovery of the colony at Kai-fung-foo by the Protestant missionaries, and the acquisition by them of a portion of their literature, excited some attention.

When my lamented father, the late Chief Rabbi, became aware of the condition of the colony, he addressed himself to the Board of Deputies with a view to their taking up

---

[1] As regards the headings of the columns in the six notable instances ב"ה ש'מ':—

    Instead of יהודה אתה יודך they have יששכר חמר גרם Gen. xlix. 14.
              ,,      שמר לך    ,,   ,,  שוטטים ושוטרים Deut. xvi. 18.
              ,,    ,,  מה טב אהלך  ,,  ,,  מוצא שפתיך תשמר Deut. xxiii. 24.

the cause of our forlorn brethren. I imagine that the Taiping rebellion was the cause of the Board not taking any active steps in the matter.

A Jewish association was formed in 1852 in the United States for the encouragement of Jewish missions to distant and neglected settlements. Funds were collected, and it was stated that Judah Touro left a legacy of $5,000 to the Society. Subsequently the Rev. Dr. Gutheim felt inclined to send out a mission, but the Civil War in the United States stopped the enterprise.

In 1864 the Jewish traveller, Benjamin II, visited England; and he expressed his readiness to visit the settlement [1]. I had the honour of being chosen hon. secretary of a Society formed to carry out the scheme. Mr. S. D. Sassoon was appointed the president of this Society, and the late Mr. L. L. Cohen accepted the treasurership. On the committee were Mr. F. D. Mocatta, Dr. Kalisch, Messrs. L. M. Rothschild and Maurice Beddington. The appeal we then issued will be found in the *Jewish Chronicle*, April 29, 1864.

Unfortunately Benjamin caught a chill in London—it was in the month of March, 1864—and died. My father then addressed himself to a branch of the firm of David Sassoon and Co. at Shanghai, and suggested that some youths from the colony might be taken in hand by them and, after preliminary training, be sent to Europe to be educated, and to return to the colony to take up the position of Jewish ministers. But this attempt too proved abortive. Two young men were actually selected and brought to Shanghai, but they soon became homesick and returned to their native place.

The next information about the colony reached us through the medium of the *New York Times*, which published the Journal of Dr. A. P. Martin, in which he gives an account of his journey to the colony. It took him nearly a month to cover the 470 miles, the distance from Pekin to Kai-

---

[1] J. J. Benjamin II, *Eight Years in Asia and Africa*. Hanover, 1863.

fung-foo. The article has been republished in his book called *A Cycle of Cathay*[1].

His adventures on the way make interesting reading. Arrived at Kai-fung-foo at last, he came to an open square, in the centre of which stood a solitary stone. On one side was an inscription commemorating the erection of the synagogue. On the other, a record of its rebuilding; but the ruins round about told a sad tale of decay and ruin. The representatives of six out of the surviving seven clans came round him, and with shame and grief confessed that their beautiful house had been demolished by their own hands. They had yielded to necessity, and disposed of the timbers and stones to obtain relief for their bodily wants. No doubt the Tai-ping rebellion had told sadly upon the town of Kai-fung-foo, and the Jews, owing to the nature of their occupations, had been the greatest sufferers. Many of them had moved away to other places.

In July, 1867, a Jew named J. L. Liebermann visited the city. He wrote a long Hebrew letter of what he saw to his father in Bielitz. This letter was translated by Dr. Löwy, and appeared in the report of the Anglo-Jewish Association for 1879. It was republished in the *Jewish Chronicle* of July 11, 1879. Another letter appeared in the same journal from a correspondent, dated Kai-fung-foo, May, 1888. It had taken the traveller five weeks on foot to get thither from Pekin. In vain he tried to gain admission into the city. He found the inhabitants of the district exceedingly fanatic, and, as now, showed hatred of strangers; his Manchu fellow traveller, however, was able to visit the city. He, as well as Mr. Dennis J. Mills, who visited the spot in 1891, give the same sad tale about the state of the Jews[2].

More recent information is that derived from an article which appeared on January 12 last in the *American Hebrew*, taken from the *Chicago Inter-Ocean* of December 31.

---

[1] Edinburgh and London, 1896.
[2] *China's Millions*, vol. XVI, No. 4. London, 1891.

The article is written by an officer in the German army stationed at Kiatschau, of the name of Herr Lehmann—not Herr J. J. Liebermann, as wrongly given.

On June 10 last my brother, the Chief Rabbi, received two interesting communications with regard to the Chinese Jews, the one from Mr. Lewis Moore and the other from Mr. S. J. Solomon, both merchants at Shanghai. It appears that the Shanghai community had been stirred to action by the fact that the Jesuits in Zikawei had brought a scroll of the Law from the Jews of Kai-fung-foo, which was exhibited at Shanghai, and subsequently sent on to Paris. Soon after a letter reached the community, which I had addressed to Sir Edward Sassoon on February 9 last, invoking his aid and that of his firm towards the rescuing of the Orphan Colony from total extinction. Meetings were held and it was decided to collect reliable information from friends in the interior of China. By this means it was ascertained that a few hundred Jews still exist at Kai-fung-foo and the surrounding districts, but that they are Jews in name alone. They cannot read a word of Hebrew, do not keep the Sabbath, or indeed observe any of our Laws; they have no teacher and no synagogue, and they intermarry with Mohammedans and heathens. A correspondent from Honan wrote:—

I learn that on the Jews coming over here, many hundreds of years ago, there were eight houses or branches bearing the names Li, Chang, Ai, Chao, Tuh, Shih, Kao.

Two of the families bore the name of Li.

These clans still exist, numbering about forty houses and about 140 persons. These are all in Kai-fung-foo. There are also scattered about in some parts a few, but not very many; their condition, socially, is not very high. Once they were the richest and most influential people in the place, but through internal dissension they have dwindled down until now they are very poor, and, I am sorry to add, have not a very good reputation. One of them is a Buddhist priest, and is in the position of a small mandarin—that is, he manages the affairs of all the other priests; it was his brother who came to see me.

Of the knowledge of their religion, I think they have not very much; I do not think the majority of them know the origin of their name.

The people belong to the "Teaou-kin-keaou," i. e. the "Pick-out-sinew" religion, after the incident mentioned in Genesis, chap. xxxii, verses 24 to 32. When I turned up the Bible and showed him the account, and explained the origin of their name, he was much interested.

I went and saw the place where once a beautiful synagogue stood, but now it is a water-hole with a stone standing alongside, a solitary witness to the one true God; on this stone the names of Abraham, Moses, Adam, &c., are mentioned, with an account of their religion. This man who came to see me promised to get me an impression of it, and if I do get it I could send you a copy. This, it is believed, is not the original stone, but one which has been put up some 200 years ago; the other one is built into the wall of some house—this man knows where it is.

They do not observe any of the ordinances of their religion, neither do they, with the exception of the Buddhist priest, observe the idolatrous practice of the heathen; they do, however, intermarry with them.

As to whether any of them could be induced to go down to Shanghai, I am unable to form an opinion, but one could find out by inquiries. With regard to your going out to Kai-fung-foo on a mission of investigation, I think it could be managed, provided you did so under "native conditions"!

Mr. S. J. Solomon further states that he had been informed that a certain Colonel Lehmann who is in the German army, and who was in Kiatschau, had been a few months ago in a place about 100 miles south-west of Kai-fung-foo, where there were about 500 native Jews, most of whom were engaged in the silk piece goods trade.

This information is confirmed by a letter received from the secretary of the Shanghai branch of the Royal Asiatic Society. Under date November 18, 1899, he writes:—

The Jewish colony has spread to other towns. Their occupation as silk weavers took some of them to a distance. Some families were well-to-do through connexion with this trade. One of the moderately large towns near Kai-fung-foo, where there is a colony of Jews, is called Tang-chwang. It is a mile and a half long, and is about 100 miles south-west of Kai-fung-foo. The Jews are all people well to-do.

They weave the silk fabric called ling, and take it or send it to Pekin.

On March 13 this year the following letter was written in Hebrew and dispatched, together with a Chinese translation (made by Dr. Jedkins of the I. M. Customs), through the channel of certain trustworthy agents residing in the interior of China:—

To the remnant of the Jewish community of Kai-fung-foo by the members of the Jewish congregation in Shanghai.

We address you, brethren in faith, having heard that in days gone by you had a synagogue at Kai-fung-foo, and ministers who taught you the ordinances and laws, how to worship the Lord God of Israel. We now learn that your House of Worship is destroyed, and that you have no Rabbi or teacher to instruct you, and to show you the way wherein you should walk as prescribed by the law of Moses, and as we are exhorted by the prophets and Ezra the scribe.

We are told that you have forgotten everything, and have gone so far as, three or four months ago, to have sold a scroll of the Law, which our own eyes have seen in the hands of those that are not of the seed of Israel. And we are further told that you are about to dispose of three or four more scrolls because you are in dire distress, and urge as your excuse that you and your children cannot read.

Now, verily, sorrow and anxiety filled our hearts when we heard these evil tidings, that affliction and want have brought you to this pass, so that Sabbath and festivals are forgotten, and that you are becoming mixed up with the heathen around you, and that you forsake the covenant, and the way your forefathers have walked for 2000 years in this land of your settlement. Tidings such as these caused the ears of every one of us that heard to tingle, and we have roused ourselves to come to your help.

Some of us were willing to come to you to find out wherefore all this evil has befallen you, and to see what we could do to heal the breach. But we are told that there would be danger to us on the way, and that if we did come in your midst, our presence would rouse anger and excite the Gentiles among whom you dwell, therefore we decided to write to you this epistle, and to ask you to send us an answer, either by letter or by word of mouth, through a member of your community.

Now, we assure you that we are eager to help you according to our ability, so that you may walk again in the footsteps of your forefathers. If you desire to rebuild the House of God, which is now become a waste place, we will collect money and send it to you; if you want a teacher to instruct you, we will send you one; if it should please you to come hither and settle here in the city of Shanghai, we will help you to do so, and put you in the way to earn a livelihood by starting you in trade, and all that you may require we will endeavour to supply you with, for there are in this city men of our faith—great and wealthy, men of affairs and business, who can help you to maintain yourselves and your sons and daughters.

Therefore we beg you not to part with the scrolls still left to you. On this letter reaching you, send two or three men to us whom we may question, and from whom we can find out what we can do for you. We will pay all the expenses of the messengers; we will give them their sustenance, and pay them their expenses until they reach again your city.

Signed in the city of Shanghai this 3rd day of the week, the 12th day of Adar II, 5660 A. M.

Signed by S. J. SOLOMON,
DAVID EZEKIEL ABRAHAM,
And forty-four other members of the Jewish community in Shanghai.

I have now brought the matter up to the position in which it stands to-day. We can but hope that this letter, with its generous offer, will reach its destination, and that, despite the present gloomy outlook of Chinese affairs, the Orphan Colony may yet at the eleventh hour be saved from assimilation or extinction.

MARCUS N. ADLER.

22 CRAVEN HILL, LONDON.

# THE HISTORY

of the

# JEWS IN CHINA

I. The Jews in China. General View.

II. The Jewish Memorial Stones and their Lesson.

BY

**S. M. PERLMANN.**

„הִנֵּה אֵלֶּה מֵרָחוֹק יָבֹאוּ
וְהִנֵּה אֵלֶּה מִצָּפוֹן וּמִיָּם
וְאֵלֶּה מֵאֶרֶץ סִינִים"

(ישעיה מ"ט י"ב)

"Behold these shall come from far,
and these from the north and from
the west;
And these from the Land of Sinim"

(Isaiah 49. 12)

To

Dr. GEORGE PERLMANN

DEDICATED

WITH PATERNAL LOVE

BY

THE AUTHOR.

London, October 1st, 1912.

A Chino-Jewish Family.

# The History of the Jews in China.

## GENERAL VIEW.

IT is a well-known fact that there have been Jews settled in China since time immemorial, but regarding the actual date of their immigration, which way they took, and what trick of fortune had led them thither, we lack all accurate historical information, and all theories made about it must be taken as being only conjectural. Curiously enough no Jewish writer had occupied himself until recently with the Chinese Jews, not even Benjamin of Tudela, although he mentions China in his works, and notwithstanding that he wrote very much about the Jews living scattered all over the world.

The first reliable records of Jews in China we find with the Tartar travellers of the ninth and fourteenth centuries.[1] Ibn-Batuta reports that many Jews have perished through massacres in

---

1) See "Ancient accounts of India and China, by two Mohammedan Travellers, translated from the Arabic by Eusebius Renandot," London, 1733

Kanfu (now Kanpin) [1]; John of Monto Corrina and Marignolli mention Jews living at Cambulac (now Peking); Marco Polo first mentions Jews in connection with the war between Kublai-Khan and his relative Nayan. The Hieromonach Alexei Winogradoff in his Istoria Biblii na Wostoke, St. Petersburg, 1895, says, "It is very likely that Jews as travellers frequented China at the time of the Kings of Israel". He points to the fact that among the folklore of the Jews in China there is a popular poem referring to the presents sent by Hyram to David (2 Sam. V. 11) as coming from an Emperor of China. But we must not overlook the oldest record which we find in the second Isaiah, who, to conclude from his prophecy on Cyrus (Chap. XLV), was a contemporary of Cyrus the Great i. e. about 530 B. C. Isaiah prophesies in chapter XLIX, 12: "These shall come from far, and these from the north and from the west and these from the land of Sinim," whereby no doubt China (Sina) is meant, as Manasseh-ben-Israel translates it.[2]

---

1) See "The Travels of Ibn-Batuta, from the Arabic by Rev. Dr. Lee", London, 1829.

2) See מקוה ישראל, פרק ו' אות כ"ד where we find the following paragraph: (מ"ט י"ב) ולפי דעתו דבר הנביא ישעיה מזה, "הנה אלה מרחוק יבאו ואלה מצפון ומים ואלה מארץ סינים, וגם בטלמיוס בס' ז' פ"ג קורא מדינת כינא, רעגיום סינארום" וזהו האמת ולא כמו שפירש ראב"ע סינים לשון סנה והוא מארץ מצרים כי הוא טעות גמור."

And despite the Septuagint's translation by "Persia" and despite the translation of the Vulgate by " the Land of the South," which is followed by Targum Jonathan, Raschi and Redak, we can take the prophecy of Isaiah as a proof that Jews were already settled in China prior to the erection of the second Temple by Zorobabel, and the re-establishment of the Jewish commonwealth by Ezra.

According to early records the Jewish population in China was estimated to amount to several thousands of souls, and James Finn (The Jews in China, London 1843) considers them as immigrants from Chaldea because of their being in possession of fragments of the Prophets Zachariah and Malachi, and their knowing several Talmudic rites. The Jews themselves, as far as their traditions go, asseverate that their ancestors immigrated into China at the time of the Han Dynasty, i. e. towards the end of the reign of Ming-ti of the East-Han Dynasty, which lasted from 25 till 221 c.e. This Emperor reigned from 58 to 75 c.e. and is renowned for having introduced Buddhism into China.

In the annals of the Mongolian Dynasty for the years 1329 and 1354, at the time when the Mongolian power began to dwindle away, Jews are mentioned as having been summoned to come to Peking to assist the imperial army, and in both documents they are named Dju-Hudu (Yehudim). Most certainly they were then numerous and of great influence, and their assistance with men and means was considered by the Government as a support to be reckoned with, since they were summoned along with the Mohammedans, who numbered many millions of souls even as far back as the 14th century. It is regrettable that the annals omit to say where the Jews were living then. What we historically know is, that during the last three centuries they lived at Kaifung the chief town of the Honan Province, where, seemingly they were to be found already prior to that time.

While the Jews were still forming communities and congregations of their own, they were known as "Tiao—kin—Kiao" which means "The Sect who extract the Sinew which shrank" (Genesis 32 33). De Guignes says, they were named also "Lan-mao-hwui-tze" meaning "Mohammedans with blue caps" because of the blue caps they used to wear in the Synagogues when praying. But probably it was only a local denomination for discriminating the Jews from the Mohammedans, as nowhere do we find it mentioned by other travellers, nor did the Jews I spoke to, know anything about it. The Jews I interviewed, only knew themselves to be descendants of the "Sect who extract the Sinew".

In the year 1704 a copious description of the

Jews at Kaifung was issued by the Jesuit Gozani, who names them also "the sect who extract the sinew" (Tiao-kin-Kiao). He adds quotations to prove that the "Tsing-chin-tze" which means "the pure and true temple", consisted of a complex of four courts and some adjoining houses destined for praying, working and dwelling. The "Li-pai-tze" i.e. the Synagogue (from the name "Li-pai" (week) it is to be concluded that they assembled there for prayer only once a week, presumably on Saturdays), measured 60 by 40 feet, having as an entrance an adorned portico of a double row of four columns. In the centre of the hall between rows of pillars there was erected a high chair covered with embroidered cushions, on which the Jews used to put the Thora scroll when reading in it before the assembled congregation. They called it "the chair of Moses". Above the chair of Moses an embroidered canopy was suspended as a token of honour, and attached to it was a tablet bearing on it the name of the Emperor in gilded letters. Beyond this tablet there was written in Hebrew

שמע ישראל יהוה אלהינו יהוה אחד.
ברוך שם כבוד מלכותו לעולם ועד.

On a gate near-by there was written also in Hebrew

ב"כ"י"כ יהוה אלהי האלהים ואדוני
האל הגדול הגבור והנורא.

The meaning of the initials ב"כ"י"כ are quite

enigmatical, and many a student has tried in vain to dissolve it satisfactorily. Tichsen considers it to mean ברוך ה' כל אם כי but that would be without a meaning here. Bratier supposes, that as the letters were to a certain degree effaced by age it would be better to put the words בין ב"ה instead of בכ"יב, but in this version also can I see no suitable meaning. My opinion is that only one letter has been slightly effaced and instead of בכ"יב we ought to read בכ"ים the initials of ברוך כבוד יהוה ממקומו No doubt another word at the end of the verse has been effaced as well, and it ought to be read ואדני האדנים as the verse in Deut. 10, 17 reads. (See Keglers Beschreibung, Edition Murr, Halle 1806) The Jews showed Gozani their Holy Scriptures; they led him into the Synagogue, even into the "Tien-Tang", i.e· "the House of Heaven" (God), situated on the west side of the temple, the side turned towards Jerusalem. This room, square in outward shape, but rounded within, was reserved for the Rabbi alone, and no other was generally permitted to enter it. Here, upon separate tables, stand twelve Thora-rolls, in honour of the twelve sons of Jacob the patriarchs of the twelve tribes of Israel. Besides these, there was one Thora-roll in the centre in honour of Moses, and each roll was enclosed in a tent of silk stuff. Gozani says that benevolence seems to have been exercised by the Jewish communities in China, and that they were living in peace and concord. On the north side of the Synagogue-yard, which measured 100 by 50 feet, there was a reserved place where the sinews of the slaughtered cattle were extracted under the supervision of a competent person commissioned for it. There was also an ancestral hall (Tze-tang); in accordance with Chinese customs they worshipped there the manes of the deceased saints or heroes of the Bible. They performed this ceremony twice a year, at the vernal and autumnal equinoxes. There were in the hall only tablets bearing the inscriptions of the names of the heroes, but no images. There were also censers where incense was burnt in honour of Abraham, Isaac, Jacob and his twelve sons, and of Moses, Joshua and Ezra. I must add, although this custom is hardly compatible with Jewish law, it may be excused when taking into consideration that the censers were presented to them by the Emperor (of the Ming Dynasty, 1368—1644 A.D.) and it was the Emperor himself who gave them the necessary instructions for burning the incense; and after all it was not used for idolatrous purposes. When the Jews entered the Synagogue they put off their shoes, and when reading in the Thora scroll the reader covered his face, immitating Moses (Exod 34,33). No Talith was used by them; they only covered their heads with blue turbans and threw red shawls over their right shoulder and tied it beneath their left arm. The blue turbans were probably meant to signify a remembrance of "T'kheleth", and to point out a difference between them and the Mohammedans, who wear white turbans when at prayer. At that time they still circumcised their newborn sons, they still observed the laws, and kept holy the feasts of Passover and Sukkoth, and especially the Day of Atonement. The name of "Jahveh" they did not pronounce, substituting for it "Adonai" (like the Jews in the West) They were always strictly monotheistic, and monotheism was their only dogma. But their pure monotheistic creed did not prevent them from believing in the existence of good and evil spirits. They believed also in a hell for the punishment of the wicked, and in a heavenly paradise as a place destined for rewarding the righteous. In praying they turned their faces to the West, the side of Jerusalem. They had also many customs and rites like those of the Western Jews, and the same calendar.

We find in the course of centuries many other references to the Jews in China by travellers and missionaries, although Chinese literati only very seldom and briefly mention Jews in their works. The first Chinese to mention Jews was Sung-tze-an in his work "Tung-king-ke" (written during the rule of the Shung Dynasty, 420-478 A.D.). He speaks of a house at Kaifung set apart for prayers to the heavenly spirit. The second Chinese man of letters mentioning Jews was Weih-Shuh, who writes about a foreign Temple of Heaven at Chang-ung in Shen-si Province, which it is said was erected in 621 A D.

As it may be concluded from many sources, there were in the 15th century many Jewish congregations in China, including one at Ningpo, one at Hang-chew and one in Peking.

Pater Matteo Ricci, the most learned, most conscientious and most prominent Jesuitic missionary, who arrived in China in the last quarter of the 16th century (1581 C.E. and died at Peking in the year 1610) in his report to the Vatican, gives an account of his first discovering Jews in China. He writes: At the commencement of the 17th century a Chinese came to his house telling him, he called because as he was told that foreigners had arrived in Peking, who worship the Only One God and are not Mohammedans, he was eager to verify whether the rumour was true or not. Pater Ricci says, he recognised the man at once as not being of the Mongolian race. He led him into the Mission House Chapel and in his presence kneeled down before two images, one showing the Madonna with the child Jesus and John the Baptist, and the other showing the four apostles. The Chinese kneeled down also, and afterwards said "We in China adore our deceased ancestors. One of the images, I am sure, shows Rebecca and her two sons Jacob and Esau, but what is the meaning of the second picture, why does it only show four sons of Jacob when there were twelve? In an intimate conference after this incident, Pater Ricci was told by his guest, that his name was Nagi, and was a Jew who had come from Kaifung to Peking for the great examinations. He further told him that there were twelve Jewish families living in Kaifung who had a nice synagogue and a Thora scroll over four hundred years old. He said, that besides the Jewish community at Kaifung there were many Jewish families at Hang-Chow, the chief town of Chekiang, who had a synagogue as well, and that many Jews were settled all over China. Pater Ricci produced to his visitor a Bible, but he was only able to make out the letters. He confessed that for his neglecting the Hebrew language, giving preference to Chinese he had many a time been rebuked by the Rabbi. Pater Ricci was very interested in all the Jew related to him, and sent out to Kaifung for particular information finding all and everything corroborated. Afterwards more Jews visited him. Pater Ricci then sent, through a converted Chinese, a message to the Rabbi at Kai-fung-fu giving therein explanations to everything he had said in the conferences he had had with Nagi, chiefly trying to convert the Rabbi by enlightening him in telling him that the, by the Jews eagerly hoped for and expected Messiah, had already appeared in the bodily person of Jesus of Nazareth, who brought salvation not only to the Jews, but to the heathens as well by converting them into Christians. The Rabbi promptly replied that he refused to accept the recognition of the Christian Messiah, saying it was erroneous to believe it as, forsooth, the Messiah has not yet appeared, and would come in the matured time, some ten thousand of years later. But,—continued the Rabbi in his answer to Pater Ricci—as from all the reports which had reached him, he had gained a thorough conviction of Pater Ricci's great and profound knowledge, he—the Rabbi—was willing and ready to cede his rabbinical office to Pater Ricci on the conditions that Pater Ricci should take up his residence in Kaifung-fu among the congregation there, and should promise to abstain furthermore from eating pork,

From this correspondence exchanged between the Rabbi and Pater Ricci, we may quite clearly infer that at that time (in the beginning of the 17th century) the Jews in China had only a faint conception of the Jewish religion and surely were already nearly absorbed by the Chinese. It undoubtedly proves the Jews to have been thoroughly imbued with Chinese views on abstract religion, as to consider it no obstacle to install a believer in Christ in the post of a Rabbi, if he only abstained from eating pork, taking his believing in Christ as a valueless superstition not worth any attention.

I consider it as important to aver that all records of Pater Ricci ought to be taken as historical documents, as he established his reputation as a staunch truth-loving man of broad views by fearlessly stating in his reports to the Vatican the erroneous means and ways adopted by the other Missionaries in trying to convert the Chinese to Christianity. He, although himself a devout Christian, did not allow his religiousness to mislead him to partiality, he did not hesitate even to mention in his records all the preferences he detected in the religions of China, and for doing so he was prosecuted and denounced by the Dominicans, who accused him of being on the verge of becoming a renegade, and instead of converting the Chinese to Christianity it was to be feared that he would become a proselyte to Buddhism. His behaviour strongly displeased and irritated the Pope, and Pater Ricci was ordered to leave China at once, but the recalling order reached China in the year 1610 when he died.

In the year 1613 Julius Aleni visited the Jews at Kaifung, and in 1642 Samedi recorded that Jews were living in four towns in China and very much esteemed by their neighbours. And that in Nanking he was informed by a Mohammedan, that in that city he knew four families of Jews who had embraced the religion of the Koran, they being the last of their race there, and their instructors having failed as their numbers diminished.

No records reached us afterwards till the Bishop Smith of Shanghai sent out (in 1850) two Chinese converts to Kaifung in order to investigate the condition of the Jews there. But as the Chinese emissaries were ignorant of the Hebrew language, they were only instructed how to copy Hebrew letters, and all they could obtain was, to bring with them some fragments of the Bible and of prayers of an ancient date, written on vellum. The late Marcus Adler in his "Chinese Jews" concludes from the said prayers that the Chinese Jews followed the Maimonides in the same way as do the Jews in Yemen. Dr Neubauer wrote explanations to these prayers in the Jewish Quarterly Review, Vol. VIII, and Mr. Elkan Adler gave supplements to it in the said J.Q R, Vol. X. Both the late Marcus Adler and Mr. Elkan Adler (in his נגוי פרס ומדי) prove very convincingly that in the last 300 years the Jews of China were in religious matters under the influence of the Jews of Persia. But nothing can be inferred from it as to the religious influence on them in the earlier centuries.

The great inundation of 1849 swept away the synagogue at Kaifung, and caused also very great loss to the Jewish community, amounting then to some 200 souls. The impoverishment of the congregation, and the destruction of their synagogue was the cause of splitting up the community; they neglected the education of their children, the Hebrew language fell into oblivion, and not even one of them was able to read Hebrew; they then disposed of their houses, and most of them emigrated into the neighbouring provinces.

The critical period for China, the time of the Taiping rebellion (1860—64), gave a moral blow to the Kaifung Jews; they suffered severely by the great inundation in 1860, and were decimated by massacres; they then became thoroughly disorganised in every way. But they still followed some of the time-honoured and sacred commands; they still continued to extract the sinew, they abstained from eating pork and married only in their own tribe. They were very jealous not to be confounded with Mohammedans, and if one tried to take them for such, because the Mohammedans also abstain from pork and do circumcise their sons, the Jews were anxious to disprove it.

In 1866, Rev. Martin, the President of the Tsung-wan College in Peking, went to Kaifung for investigating personally the condition of the Jews. He writes (A Cycle of Cathay, Chicago 1896): By certain reasons we may presume that some centuries ago many Jewish families were living in China, and it is still remembered that a synagogue at Ningpo which is now ruined, has presented two Thora scrolls to the synagogue of Honan. Rev. Martin could detect nothing of importance. He saw some 6 Jews, members of the 7 families still living there (as he was told). But as Rev. Martin, according to his own report, has committed the blunder of telling them that he had mastered the Hebrew language, and was well versed in the Hebrew Holy Scriptures, but when the Jews brought to him a Thora scroll and found him unable to read in it, he was exposed and ridiculed. It is most probable that the Jews distrusted him and kept reserved. Moreover, it is evident from his report that, in his capacity as a Christian missionary, he tried to preach Christianity to them, aiming to make converts of them. No wonder then that through his agitatory calling which is much suspected, hated and abused all over China, he quite naturally caused the Jews to look askance at him, and to avoid entering into closer explanations or giving him candid information. Still it is worth noting what Rev. Martin records. He mentions, that two of the Jews were dressed in official attire, one had a golden button, the other a crystal one on their hats (marks of having passed certain examinations required for becoming a candidate for government office). One of them was the son of a Rabbi, who died some 30 years prior to that time, and with whom the last expert of the Hebrew language at Kaifung was buried. The Jews there, still possessed some Thora scrolls as relics only, as nobody was capable of reading in them. The Jews, feeling themselves cut off from their tribe and about to become extinct altogether intended to exhibit a Thora scroll on the market place in order to draw the attention of Jewish travellers, hoping to find assistance from their Western brethren, and to be instructed anew in the holy language.

Rev. Martin found that the Jews did not follow Jewish rites, and did not even circumcise their newborn sons, and were no longer acquainted with the Hebrew tongue. The only remainder of the synagogue was a tablet bearing in gilded letters the inscription "Israel", that was formerly fixed at the entrance of the synagogue; it was afterwards placed in the Mohammedan mosque. Therefore some of the Jews go to the mosque for prayer.

In 1869 Professor Martin wrote to the "Jewish Times" of New York, telling that, the rebuilding of the synagogue is indispensable to give this moribund colony a bond of union, and that without this, nothing can save it from extinction, but the appeal excited some discussion among the Jews' but produced no further result. In 1872 some of them moved from Kaifung to Peking, hoping to find support there, but they became soon aware that their expectations were vain, and returned to their homes. He further records that he met the Jews on the site where the synagogue had formerly stood, and there, in the middle of the place he still found a memorial stone bearing on one side a date corresponding to 1164, and on the other to the date 1488, showing the respective dates of the erection and restoration of the synagogue. (See Part II. The Jewish Memorial Stones and their Lesson.)

Alexei Winogradoff mentions also this memorial stone and says : from some additional characters in the inscription it may be concluded that Jews have been in China even at so early a date as before Moses (!). He mentions also the memorial stone of the same synagogue of the year 1511, on which there is an inscription defining the Jewish religion as strictly monotheistic. The Most High is here called "Tao" and this denomination for

God is often repeated. I take it as a proof that at that time the Jews already commenced to assimilate to the Chinese and named the Only One God by the name "Tao" in accordance with the greatest philosopher of China "Lao-tze" in his immortal book "Tao-teh-king. Surely a purer and higher abstract philosophical conception of God as comprehended by "Lao-tze" in his "Tao-teh-king" is inconceivable, but, although his teaching is purely monotheistic and may suit a mind thoroughly trained in high philosophy, it is too high to be apprehended by the bulk of a nation, nor could it be properly understood by the Jews in China. The Jewish biblical designation "Jahveh" for the One God of Israel and of the whole world, ought not to be translated except in the way we do, always maintaining its connection with the Bible, having, when translating it into other languages always "Jahveh" in mind. But such was not the case when rendered by "Tao" a name taken from a philosopher who never thought, heard or knew of the name "Jahveh". The Jews, by adopting this translation really changed their monotheistic creed, with "Jahveh" as the Only God into another alien creed, with "Tao" as the Only God, and although this creed was also monotheistic, still it was the first step to abandoning their own faith by which they were the chosen people of God, and becoming absorbed by another faith taught by a greater nation than they were. The English Missionary, Mr. Dennis I. Mills, who has been to Kaifung-fu some 18 years ago, writes in the "China's Millions" for March 1897, that he had the opportunity of conversing with one of their (the Jews') prominent men (?). And—he proceeds—enquiring as to any remaining copies of their Scriptures, he informed us that the only one remaining was in his possession, many having been spoilt by damp. "One", he said, "about eighty years ago, had, during a violent storm been carried by the wind, right into heaven—and from that time" he added, "our religion began to decline".

About seven or eight years ago, members of three or four Jewish families came over from Kaifung to Shanghai, where they were taken care of, and provided by their co-religionists with means for a temporary living, and by degrees some of them were instructed in handicrafts and some were employed as office boys. As none of them had any education, they were unsuited to fill better positions. Simultaneously with the instruction given them in secular subjects, they were also instructed in Hebrew, and in the tenets and rites of the Hebrew law.

When staying at Shanghai I invited some of them to a house of a friend of mine for an interview. It is still fresh in my memory how amazed were the faces of the Chinese boys in the service of my friend, when they saw that all the ladies and gentlemen who had gathered there for this spectacle, treated these poor Chinese (Jews) as guests, taking a keen interest in them and inviting them to take seats round the same table and to have tea in company with us. The Chinese boys could not overcome their curiosity and asked the Chinese Jews what was the reason for their being so distinguished. The Chinese Jews were proud to tell them that we all, like themselves, were members of one tribe ("Brethren" as the Chinese usually call members of the same tribe), that we were all of the Jewish nation and creed, all descendants of Abraham (or as they spelt it "Ab-lo-hom" because of not being able, like all Chinese, to pronounce the "r" and substituting it by "l").

I was at once convinced that my interview, for which I had been longing for so long, would not be so productive and instructive as I had hoped; it was very apparent that the visitors were of low intellect and lacked education. It was too much to expect these people to understand how deep an interest is taken in the Chinese Jews by their co-religionists, as well as by sociologists in the West. I was disillusioned, but tried to make the best of it, and to get as much information as possible. They told me, they had come to Shanghai from Kaifung, and that there were still about one thousand Jewish souls living at Kaifung. They name themselves "Tiao-kin-kiao" i.e. "the sect who extract the sinew" and know no other name. To my question, whether they are aware that Jews in other Chinese provinces were denominated as "Lan-mao-hwui-tze" i.e "Mohammedans with blue turbans", they replied that they were ignorant of it. They proceeded to tell me, that they abstain from pork, extract the sinew from the slaughtered cattle, and mostly marry among their own tribe, but that all other Jewish rites and customs have come into oblivion ; even circumcision of their newborn sons is not exercised any more. They bury their deceased in coffins, but of a different shape than those of the Chinese are made, and do not attire the dead in secular clothes as the Chinese do, but in linen. Of the Jews I have interviewed, the older ones and little ones have been circumcised at Shanghai, but the two lads of seventeen and fifteen were opposed to the operation, and remained uncircumcised. I produced a Bible ; they were able to read in it, thanks to the instructions they had received at Shanghai, as none of the Jews at Kaifung is able to read Hebrew. I asked them to translate the first verse of Genesis ; this they did, and translated "Elohim" by "Tien" and "Hashomaim" also by "Tien". I was told that by "Tien the creator" "God" is to be understood, whereas by the "created Tien" the visible "heaven" is meant. The Chinese designation "Shang-ti" for "God" they used as well, and they told me "Shang-ti" can only be used to point out "God", never can it be used to designate by it the visible "sky", whereas "Tien" can be used for "God" and for "heaven" or "sky" alike. This explanation is quite conformable to the conceptions of all Chinese. I asked them whether they knew about two memorial stones, which, it is said, were still at Kaifung at the place where the synagogue had once been standing, and I was told that they had heard only about one (that mentioned in the Chinese Repository of 1164 and 1488). The physiognomies of the Jews I interviewed were quite Chinese, the eyes of a narrow shape, broad cheek-bones and yellow-hued faces, except one youth of seventeen, whose face had something of the peculiar Jewish type. His eyes and cheek-bones were more like those of a European, and had he not worn Chinese clothes, with shaved forehead and queue, nothing could betray him to be Chinese, except the yellow hue of his face. In their external appearance they were by no means to be distinguished from other Chinese; they shave their foreheads, wear queues, attire themselves in the same clothes as other Chinese, even the Jewish woman has crippled feet like the other Chinese women in North China. I used to meet afterwards, in the course of years, some Chinese said to be descendants of Jews. I would meet them at Chinese restaurants, in Peking and Tientsin, where no pork is served. (There are in China many sects who abstain from pork.) They told me that they were said to be descendants of Jews, but now they are Chinese in every respect without having the slightest idea what it means to be a Jew.

I quoted above the daring and improbable assumption of the Hieromonach Alexei Winogradoff that Jews were in China even at such an early date as before Moses. I do not share his opinion, but we must confess that it is startling and quite inexplicable why do the Chinese Jews designate themselves as "the sect who extract the sinew", thus identifying themselves with a legend of Jacob, and did not take some more historical and more important event in which the Jewish history is so rich? Why did they not call themselves names reminding the exodus of Egypt, or the glorious event on mount Sinai? Why did they not name themselves "the monotheists"? May we not infer from it that the first Chinese Jews when settled in China did not know these historical events at all, and only later immigrants brought to them the Mosaic law and rites? If anybody likes to expound it in such a way, I cannot assent to it. My opinion is that the very first Jews who came to China were a part of the exiles of the ten now lost tribes of Israel, who were followed by a greater body of exiles from Jerusalem after the destruction of the first temple, as I will explain more thoroughly in the course of my essay. But why did the Jews choose a name connected with the legend of Jacob in preference to another more important and historical name? They assumed this name, I presume, after the Mohammedan religion was introduced into China, fearing, (as the Mohammedans also boast of being descendants of Abraham, do circumcise their sons, recognise the divinity of the Bible, abstain from pork and profess monotheism) lest they, the Jews, should become confounded with the Mohammedans, and took the precaution of naming themselves after a special Jewish legend about the Patriarch Jacob, by which only the Jews are bound to fulfil a rite not exercised by the Mohammedans.

When and which way did the Jews immigrate into China? This is a problem to which nobody can undertake to give a satisfactory solution, but so far as we are able to conclude from accessible sources, we may take most of them to be the descendants of the ten lost tribes of Israel, and BAINBRIDGE so certainly considered them when he supposed them to have immigrated into China about 700 B.C. (I refer to a lecture delivered by BAINBRIDGE in London some time ago) [1]

That a greater part of the lost ten tribes have settled in Afghanistan and Kabulistan we can almost take as proved, (see also Massoii Benjamin Hasheni), and no less certain is it that a considerable part of them have come to Cochin-China, and—according to the Cochin History Roll—their descendants have emigrated from there, taking their way via Persia and Media to Chinese Tartary. [2] Another part of those Jews have settled among the Chazar Tartars and formed there the highest nobility, so that all Chazarian reigning Khans were elected from the descendants of Jews. Cf. Chinese Recorder, Shanghai 1885, Vol. XVI page 47, where we read as follows:

[1] May be that at that time there were not very many Jews in China, but they immigrated in greater masses later on during the Han dynasty at the time of the destruction of the second temple, therefore the tradition of the Chinese Jews goes only as far as Mingti.

[2] See ספרא בחקותי, פרק ח' ואבדתם בגוים, רבי עקיבא אומר אילו עשרת השבטים שגלו למדי.

See also Josephus, Antiquities Book IX chap. XIV. " when Shalmaneser, &c., and transplanted all the people into Media and Persia, &c., &c.

According to Forster . . . . "The remainder of the Ten tribes, according to the Cochin History Roll, migrated through Media and Persia in the direction of Chinese Tartary, and the tribes of Simeon, Ephraim and Manasseh are represented to have settled in the country of the Chazar Tartars, when they became ferocious nomades, celebrated for their horses, and dreaded for their warfare. Moreover, the Royal Family in this great Tartar tribe were Jews, and the Chagan or King of the Chozars was always chosen from this Jewish Stock."

Forster quotes Eben Haukal's Oriental Geography to the effect that "the King of Asmed city in Khozar is a Jew, and on good terms with the Padshah of Serir." He also says: "From the sixth to the tenth century the Chazars were the lords of Central Asia."

Judging from another source I am inclined to assume that the Thibetans are partly also descendants of the lost ten tribes. George Timkowski in his "Travels of the Russian Mission through Mongolia to China," London 1827, says: "The physiognomies of the Thibetans are like the physiognomies of the Gipsies," to which the editor in a marginal note remarks, "This opinion corresponds to the observations of Thomas Maning, who also visited Lhassa, he maintains that the

Thibetan physiognomies are not of the Mongolian type but resemble more the Jewish type."

There are two customs existing in some provinces of China to which I will draw the attention of the reader, and the customs may be has some connection with the immigrated Jews in China. Alexei Winogradoff in his "Istoria Biblii na Wostoke," writes "In the provinces of Honan and Kiangsu the custom of Levirate marriages prevails, and is also to be met with, though only in single cases, in other provinces. The sources cannot be traced as to when and how this custom has come to China." As chiefly in these provinces (Kaifung is in the Honan province) the Jews were settled, it may be admitted that the Jews have brought this custom (according to Deut. 25. 5—10) with them and they still continue to adhere to it even after they had become amalgamated and assimilated with the aborigenes. And should my supposition be right, we may then infer that the Jews immigrated into China before the Talmudic time, as the first Talmudists (See Talmud-Babli, Tractat Yebamoth page 39 and 109) have abolished this custom for reasons of morality and introduced for it the "Khalitza" as compulsory, a rite allowed by Biblical law only in case of extreme need (ibid.) i.e. when the brother of the deceased refused to comply with the Levirate law, and declined to marry the widow of his deceased brother. It is, of course only a supposition, as we cannot take the Levirate custom to be exclusively of Jewish origin, for we find it also among the Mongolians (see Du Halde. Description de la Chine et de la Tartarie Chinoise. Vol. 4.). Still it could be presumed that both the Mongolians and the Chinese have taken it from the Jews, if there were not among the Indians any Levirate marriages at the time of the Rigveda, (2400 B.C. i.e. some 300 years before Abraham) as the traces of this custom are said to have been discovered in the Veda. (See Andrew Lang. Myth, Ritual and Religion, London 1887.) Moreover, Maimonides (Moreh Nebukhim III. 49) says "This custom (Levirate marriages) existed among other nations (Egyptians and Indians) before the time of Moses, (I may add in paranthesis, that among the Jews it also existed before Moses, even at the time of Jacob. See Genesis 38) and it had with them the same reason that is plainly given in the Bible, i.e. not to allow the name of the deceased brother to become extinct, and therefore the firstborn son was considered as the son of the deceased brother." I will observe by the way that Levirate marriages existed in Scotland as late as the 11th century, according to Lord Hales. (See note 4 to Ruth 4 by John Kitto).

When Herbert Spencer (Principles of Sciology) in speaking of Levirate marriages rejects the opinion of those who take it as a remainder of the old custom of poliandry, he is quite right, but I cannot agree with his hypothesis, which he even considers as very probable, that the Levirate law among the Jews may have had its origin in compelling by law the surviving brother to take care of the unprovided widow and children of his deceased brother. as it is customary with the Ostiacs. If this were the basis of the law, it would be very curious that the Jewish law has ordered the Levirate marriage in quite the contrary case. It is quite plainly and distinctly commanded (Deut. 25. 5) " If brethren dwell together, and one of them die, and have no son left, &c." which the Talmud expounded as if no "child" was left, then the Levirate law comes into force, whereas if there were children left, the surviving brother is not only not compelled to take care, either of them or of the widow, but in such a case a marriage is strictly forbidden, (Levit. XVIII. 16 and XX. 21).

The second custom which I indicated is, the abstaining of the Chinese from wearing garments mingled of animal and vegetable substances (Shatnes) a custom resembling the precept in Levit. 19. 19 and Deut. 22. 11. When I first heard from the Chinese that they withold from wearing garments mingled of animal and vegetable substances I was extremely surprised, much more than by the custom of Leviratic marriages, as the Leviratic custom may have originated from different economical causes, in different countries at different times independently from each other. In China it could have been the outcome of causes quoted by Herbert Spencer, whereas in the Jewish nation the reason was probably the one which is twice mentioned in the Bible, in Genesis 38. 8 to "raise up seed to thy brother" and in Deut. 25. 6 "And it shall be, that the first-born which she beareth shall succeed in the name of his brother which is dead, that his name be not put out of Israel," but the prohibitive command of wearing garments mingled of animal and vegetable substances it seems has not the slightest vestige of an economical origin, and still we find it with the Chinese as with the Jews. As neither in the Bible nor in the Talmud do we find any reason for this precept I hoped to find a clue to it with the Chinese, but my hope was in vain. The only answer I could get on asking for the reason of this strange custom was " we do not wear garments mingled of animal and vegetable substances " an answer which every Chinese considers as amply sufficient, because they consider as sacred every custom which is traditionally delivered to them from their forefathers, but certainly I could not be satisfied with this categorical but insignificant reply. I could not even find out whether this custom has been accepted by all Chinese, but I heard it prevails in Thibet.

James Finn also mentions this custom in his "The Jews in China," London 1843, and relates: "A cloth manufacturer in Stockport lately brought some samples of a mixed cotton and woollen cloth to a house of the same trade in Leeds. The proprietor of the latter having no occasion for the goods, and remarking that the colours were mostly suited to Asiatic taste, suggested that they might be sent to China. It was answered, they have been there already, and sold at a fair profit, but were returned in a few days by the Hong merchants, who pronounced it contrary to their religion that animal and vegetable substances should be woven together and worn."

From all this I have said and quoted it is obvious that the Chinese custom is still more severe than the Jewish law, as the first excludes also cotton from being allowed to be woven with wool, whereas the Jewish law prohibits only linen and wool to be mingled. This difference astonished me also, and I surmised that this difference may be taken as a proof that the reason for the two prohibitions also were different ones, and assuming it we shall have two insolvable riddles instead of one. But after looking into the matter more attentively I have reason to think that after all, the prohibition of both are based on the same motive. We find in the Talmud (יומא ע"א ב׳) an explanation given by R. Jossi b'rabbi Chanina that the word „בד" means a plant growing in stalks, and that excludes cotton from being prohibited to mingle with wool, because cotton grows on trees.

The reason why it has been prohibited to the Jews to mingle these two substances together is differently presumed. Josephus (Antiquit. IV. 8. 11) writes "Let not anyone of you wear a garment made of woollen and linen, for that is appointed to be for the priests alone." We may presume that Josephus being himself a descendant of the priest caste, may have known the reason by tradition, moreover the Talmud's (ערכין ג'ב׳) also says that the priests were allowed to wear a garment of mingled substances, namely was the girdle which the priests had to wear when sacrificing made of wool and linen. But Maimonides gives another reason for the prohibition of mingled substances; he says (מורה נבוכים ג׳ ל'ז׳) ". . . . this was also the motive to prohibit the wearing of clothes of wool and linen mingled together, because the priests of the heathen used to combine animal and vegetable substances in one garment."

As the Chinese like the Jews have always been monotheists, I think that both may have prohibited on the motive which is given by Maimonides, namely, to prevent heathen customs from penetrating into the habits of their nations. I will yet add that the Chinese as well as the Jews allow the garments to be woven of silk and wool, or silk and linen or cotton mingled together.

Before concluding I must add, in justice to the old civilised Chinese nation, that the Jews in China have never had to complain of intolerance; they were never under exceptional laws; they were never persecuted or despised for their religion. They always enjoyed full rights like the Chinese. No doubt the full emancipation on one side, and their having been so completely cut off from their Western co-religionists on the other side, was one of the causes of their becoming absorbed by the Chinese.

James Finn, who lived many years in China, and was afterwards British Consul at Jerusalem writes in his book "The Jews in China" "In reviewing the past ages of Israelitish sojourn in China, as well as our limited knowledge will permit, we immediately feel how happily tame is that retrospect compared with the dark and sanguinary annals of Jews in Mohammedan and Popish realms, for the toleration of the Chinese spirit has never yet discovered that the Hebrew Passover is celebrated with an appetite for human blood; and happy is the nation which, while it has had an opportunity to do so, has not persecuted them for religion's sake, because it is written, "I will bless them that bless thee, and curse him that curseth thee" (Gen. 12 3)"

Speaking about the assimilation of the Jews in China, it is impossible to avoid the question, why have the Jews been absorbed by the Chinese and not by the Christians? Surely many circumstances acting together brought about the assimilation, and I will lay before the reader my solution of this question, as a result of my study of the problem during many years of my sojourn in China.

It is unquestionably true, and would be of salutary consequences if the powerful dictators of the world would take it for guidance, that to grant unrestricted emancipation and freedom is the most practical means for making a sincere and devoted friend of an immigrated alien minority or even of a subdued nation, whereas pressure, restrictions and persecution provoke opposition and enmity. It will always remain true that the best way to conquer an enemy is to make a friend of him. China realised this truth and has always acted accordingly. China has always granted equal freedom and equal rights to everyone regardless of nationality or faith, and she has succeeded in converting the adopted strangers into true and faithful sons of their great country; witness the Cossacks captured at Albazin in 1685. China did not ill-treat the 101 soldiers and their clergyman, Maxim Leontieff, whom she brought as captives to Peking; nay, she granted them the enjoyment of the same rights and privileges as the Chinese themselves, portioned out to them fields and gardens, allowed them to profess their Orthodox creed, even permitted Russia to establish in Peking and Orthodox mission for instructing the captured soldiers in their religious precepts. The result of all that was, that notwithstanding all the endeavours Russia has made to retain the Cossacks as Orthodox Christians they became by degrees absorbed by the Chinese, and now the descendants of those Cossacks have only a faint recollection of their parents having been once Russian and Orthodox.

But freedom and emancipation alone would not be sufficient to make a cultured nation, as the Jews have been since thousands of years, abandon their faith and their nationality. The Jewish nation was in possession of Holy Scriptures declaring them to be the only beloved chosen people of God; they had a history full of heroic deeds, and were always proud of both.(*)

Now, it is true, freedom and emancipation could be sufficient to make of the immigrated alien Jews patriotic sons of China, as freedom and emancipation have made the Jews in France and England patriots heart and soul. But why have the Jews in China been assimilated and have even abandoned their religion, and have renounced their privilege to be the firstborn son of God? Why could the Jews resist the highly cultured nations of England and France and keep their own? When we see the same Jewish nation successfully defending their position on one battlefield and being thoroughly overpowered and beaten in another struggle, must we not infer from it, that

---

(*) Kant ("Die Religion," in a note to section 3. Edition 1749) says: "The reason why the Jews have not assimilated is, because a nation who is in possession of Holy Scriptures will never fuse with a nation without sacred books as the Roman Empire and the whole civilised world was at that time, having only time-honoured customs. Nay, the nation possessing written sacred books (although a conquered one) makes proselytes among their conquerors. It was the case with the Jews when they came to live among the heathen Romans, they brought with them the written law and succeeded by it to conquer spiritually the Romans, and later on the whole heathen world." Senecca deplored bitterly that the conquered Jews were dictating laws to the conquerors. (See Augustin De Civiate Dei VI. II.)

success and failure was not dependent on the power of the Jews so much as on the weapons and strength of their opponents ? Being myself a Jew I feel somewhat uncomfortable in analysing the causes and effects of these struggles, ending so differently. But it can never be humiliating to confess the truth, and I must confess that the Jewish position in the struggle against the Christians was very strong and advantageous, and on the contrary, very weak and disadvantageous against the Chinese, taking it, of course, only so far as men could judge and dared to decide themselves on the qualities of the different religions, regardless of the axiomatic truth that religion can only exist when accepted and trusted without any criticism.

When Christianity began to develop and to find disciples, the Judæo-Christians were thoroughly religious and law-abiding Jews; they strictly obeyed the Mosaic law and fulfilled every command of the Old-Testament, only in their believing Jesus to be the Messiah (Christ) did they differ from the other Jews, and when Paul decided to modify the law, to renounce so many commandments, the Judæo-Christians abused him and rejected his writings as those of an apostate. Paul was therefore urged by James, the head of the Judæo-Christians, to satisfy by an obvious action the "many thousands of Jews which believe and are zealous of the law" to convince them "that thou thyself (Paul) also walkest orderly and keepest the law" (see the Acts, XXI and Eusebius). But Paul, who was entirely a Hellenist, in thought and sentiment, as it is evident from nearly all the epistles that bear his name, did not care about their attacks, although he yielded to the demand of James; being convinced that only by syncretism was there any hope of planting Christianity among the pagans, he acted accordingly and succeeded.

The circumstances were at that time very favourable to success, as on one side the enlightened Jews were imbued with the philosophy of Alexandria, Antiochia, and Asia Minor, and were indifferent to the precepts of the Jewish law, and on the other side the moral men among the Heathens were disgusted of the mischievous immorality practised by the idolatrous pagans. Paul found support in these classes and succeeded in modifying the original Judæo-Christianity into quite a new faith after his own design, so much has he remodelled the Judæo-Christian original faith that such a renowned scholar as Professor Adolph Harnack (Das Wesen des Christenthums. Leipzig 1890) says very correctly "The real founder of Christianity was Paul," as without the concessions to the heathens by Paul, the pagans would never have agreed to be converted to Christianity. The heathens adopted the new-stamped religion, based on Jewish law tempered by compromises made to the pagan taste, as a quite new religion and were satisfied, whereas the Jews continued to look upon it as something anomalous. The Jews did not recognise Jesus either as a Saviour or as a Messiah, and so long as the Temple was not destroyed the strong-minded Jews had no desire for a Messiah, but were longing for a living, daring and fighting hero, like Judah Maccabeus, to lead them to victory without pretending to be a Messiah. These Jews naturally could not see in Jesus the ideal of a leader when he was preaching "whosoever shall smite thee on the right cheek, turn to him the other also." It was only the small community of Judæo-Christians, all in all some 500 despairing fantastical "meek and poor in spirit" who put their hope in a Messiah. Nay, the strong-minded Jews did not even consider Jesus a Rabbi of great erudition; they simply looked on Christianity as on distorted Judaism, corrupted by invented dogmas contrary to the original Jewish strict monotheism. The Jews although they have gladly adopted wordly customs and secular science from the Christians, could not assimilate and let their religion be absorbed by

Christianity, as Christianity was considered by them Judaism gone astray. The high ethical precepts of Christianity could not make any impression upon them; as they found the same moral tenets in the Bible and Talmud, they considered them as merely borrowed from the Jewish Scriptures. Time went on, Christianity became very strong, and developed into the supreme ruling power in Europe; but alas, the Jews have to tell a sad tale of the power wielded by the Popes, by the crusaders, and by all the others uneducated, uncouth and barbaric rulers, all of them pretending to be Christians. No wonder that the Jews learned to despise the professors of such a Christianity who, while chanting Jewish hymns to the Jewish God, robbed and slaughtered the Jewish people. Moreover, the Jews were always well versed in the Scriptures and generally more educated than even the Christian theologists of those dark times, and were astonished to see that the bulk of Christians had no idea at all of the origin of Christianity, and were completely ignorant of the Bible and its commandments.

In quite another position were the Jews who had immigrated into China. I must premise that I am on the side of those Sinologists who consider the Chinese to be monotheists (among them Max Müller and James Legge). The difference between the monotheism of China and the monotheism of Jews, Christians and Mohammedans is, so to say, that the former confess only the principle of monotheism, whereas the latter contend the absolute necessity of recognising also a certain monotheistic dynasty. The Chinese are for monotheism in principle, they do not care whether you agree with them to name the Only One God " Shangti " as they do, or " Jahveh " (with or without a Trinity) whereas Jews, Christians and Mohammedans not only demand the belief in monotheism, but with them it is a *conditio sine qua non* that " Jahveh " must be the Only God. (The Christians compel one moreover to believe in the Trinity).

When the first Jews, the descendants of the ten lost tribes of Israel reached China, and it took them presumably some 50—100 years to come there by the roundabout way over Afghanistan, Kabulistan, Cochin and Tartary, they naturally must have been surprised to find a great civilised nation with a history thousands of years older than their own (Yao the great reigned in China some 200 years before Abraham was born) and just those were the days of Chinese glory, when the nation was under the fresh influence of the highest philosophical doctrine of monotheism as taught by their immortal Philosopher "Lao-tze" (born 604 B.C.) who regarded any name given to the abstract idea of the Godhead as a profanation, even the name " God " he did not admit. (See Victor v. Straus's Translation of "Tao-teh-king.") And no less was the nation imbued with the refined administrative reforming notions of Confucius (born 551 B.C.) all of them based on high ethical principles. After these heroes of human learning and justice followed Mencius (180 years after Confucius) who expounded, preached and divulged the doctrines and teachings of his great master Confucius. So the Jews for the first time came face to face with a nation confessing monotheism, though without the slightest idea of " Jahveh " and of his chosen people ; [1] a nation without a nobility to grasp the best positions in the government, but giving all honour and preference to the learned man, the same as it has always been with the Jews; a nation possessing Holy Scriptures of a superior ethical quality though without pretensions to revelation, [2] but

---

[1] That the Jews in course of time, learned to consider the Chinese religion as monotheistic is proven by the inscriptions on the memorial stones (See Part II.)

[2] A precarious position impossible to defend successfully against attacks from thorough unbelievers on one side, and difficult to give a satisfactory answer to the interrogations of believers in Godhead but opposing the belief in revelations on the other side, questioning why some nations needed

only as teachings of their sages, a nation in possession of a book called "Yih-king" which served the Chinese as the "Urim-We-Thumim" did the Jews in the Biblical epoch, and is of such high philosophical value that, as proved by Dr. Paul Carus, Leibnitz had taken many a thing from it. (see Dr. Paul Carus "Chinese Philosophy" Chicago 1898) and Confucius, in the last year of his life said, if he had to live another fifty years he would devote the whole time to the study of the Yih-king. No wonder that all that stimulated the Jews to contemplation and comparisons.

To prove that the qualities mentioned were really possessed by the Chinese, I will quote some prominent authors. Thomas Taylor Meadows (The Chinese and their Rebellions, London 1856) says: "No nation can boast to possess Holy Scriptures so totally free from abusive sentences as the Chinese. Not one sentence is to be found in the Chinese Holy Scriptures which could not be read in every English family." Schopenhauer (Wille in der Natur, Sinologie) says: "For its inner excellence, for its truth and for its great

revelations when the sages of others could reach the same high moral standing by their own ethical mind, does it not mean that revelation stigmatises those nations, to whom it was granted to be of an inferior intelligence, lacking sages of common sense and high ethical preceptions?

number of professors, we have to consider this religion (Buddhism) as the most distinguished in the world." The Jesuit historian Jarric (quoted by A. R. Colquhoun in his "China in Transformation, London 1898) wrote: "If Plato could come back from Hades, he would declare that the Republic he desired had become a reality in China." The prominent Roman Catholic missionary Huc wrote about sixty years ago (Das Chinesische Reich, Leipzig 1856): "Europe is endeavouring to become (in religious matters) what China has been for thousands of years." C. F. R. Allen in his preface to the Shi-king writes: "That which made the most profound impression on me, was, in what a pure monotheism the old Chinese believed, and their bright ideas of God. He was not with them a tribal God, but the supreme Lord and the supreme ruler of the whole universe."

The astonishment of the immigrated Jews must have grown continually, seeing that all the ethical tenets which were revealed to them by God as a preference to his chosen people they found in China not only taught and commanded but practically exercised. They, the aliens, were treated with the same kindness as the Chinese themselves, and became aware of the fact that "to love his neighbour, and to love the stranger as himself," which was commanded to them by

God (Levit. XIX), and "not to do to others as one would not that it should be done to him," *) was taught to the Chinese by their sages out of righteousness and common sense. The Jews found further, that the same sages who taught the people love for their fellowmen in the highest and noblest degree (Teachings of Lao-tze and Buddha) did not teach any compulsory obligations of men to God, but left it to the discretion of every one to treat religion as a strictly private affair. Neither are the Chinese commanded to love God, nor to believe in God, nor to fulfil commandments not comprehensible to men, of which there are many in the Bible (although the commandments of the Bible certainly have their good reasons, but are not known to us); even more, one of the three founders of Chinese religion, Confucius, was himself an agnostic.

Meanwhile the Chinese continued to give to the Jews all privileges and all rights, making friends of them, and the Jews could not see any reason for keeping themselves aloof from the Chinese; they approached each other, intermarried and by degrees the more convenient religion (according to human understanding) has proved to be the fittest to survive.

---

*) Talmud Babli, Tract. Sabbath, 31. 1.

It would be a very interesting task and worth while the expense, if a competent man could be commissioned to investigate at Kaifung the present condition of the Jews still living there It would be interesting not only for the Jews as a nation but also for science in general. I am sure the half assimilated, half amalgamated Jews would at once return to their old faith if support were given to them to facilitate it. The Jews I met at Shanghai were glad and happy to work hard, finding consolation and contentment in knowing themselves to belong to the old Israelitic tribe.

# The History of the Jews in China.

## THE JEWISH MEMORIAL STONES AND THEIR LESSON.

---

Since the time when the first startling intelligences reached the West that there were Jews living in China, the searching minds of Jews and Christians alike were alive to the question of the origin of this detected Jewish branch. But, unfortunately, the obtained results have been near to nothing, as not only have the Jews there become extinct altogether, but not even copious records have remained after them, and all we have been able to procure were some faint vestiges of Jewish congregations, gleaned from engravings on memorial stones, so that when we speak of "the Jews of China" it is to be understood as "the Jews who once lived in China," as there are no more Jews in China now. There is no Jewish congregation in existence, not even one pure and unmixed Jewish family is left. Since hundreds of years the Jews have been gradually and constantly under the process of absorption, and it has strongly worked on them, so that they are now totally mingled with the Chinese masses, and even the faint traces will soon be effaced. When we now and then met a single individual who still preserved a slight glimpse of tradition to the effect of being a descendant of the Jewish race he looked on it quite indifferently, contemplating it as a passed stage of evolution, it being for him, at the most, merely a scientific problem, insignificant to him about the same as is to us the problem whether we are the degenerated descendants of progenitors who have been supermen something like angels, or whether we have improved so much, by so many evolutions as to become highly cultured scions of a low stock of apes.

From a practical point of view it would seem to be a waste of time to investigate into the causes which brought about the effect of annihilation of the large Jewish population which once flourished in China, being sure that even the breath coming from the four winds will not be vigorous enough to revive their dry bones. But the Jewish nation is at the present juncture in a most critical position, resembling a woman in throes, who although being in a dangerous state, and quite on the verge of death, is yet more likely, and in course of nature, about to bring forth new life. When from one side several barbaric countries have let loose all forces of the hell to destroy the Jewish nation, ill-treated from yore, applicating all means of felony and vileness to undermine its existence, we at the same time see on the other side a strong movement, animated by a determined will to regenerate the old depressed nation, which will not be any more content with its lot, to boast as hitherto, of having been the medium to transmit the monotheistic religion to the world, but endeavours to regain and obtain for itself a share in the materialistic world, and I do not hesitate to express my strong hope and conviction that our nation, like the woman in throes, has more right to hope a natural development to success and life than to failure and death.

Optimistic as we may be, we must, however, not leave without attention every phase of the long and sad history of our nation, but we are rather bound to take great care not to commit any blunders, lest they should become stumbling blocks to debar our path to freedom and deliverance.

From this standpoint a close study to examine the circumstances which caused the doom of our national branch in China is now more important for us than it has been since we have lost our independence some 1850 years ago.

With this purpose in mind I will herewith reproduce translations of several inscriptions on monumental tablets and memorial stones detected at Kai-fung-fu, giving a proper idea of the religious standing of faith of the Jews in China at different times. And when we sum up the inferences they will surely supply us with some valuable hints for directing our nation at the present turning-point.

### I.

### The Memorial Stone of 1164 C.E.

"Regarding the Jewish religion: Our first ancestor was Adam, our religion was founded by Abraham, afterwards Moses came, who was the mediator of the Holy Scriptures. At the time of the Han Dynasty (East-Han-Dynasty, 25 till 221 C.E.) this religion was introduced in China. In the second year of Hias Tsung (1164. Sung Dynasty) a synagogue was erected at Kaifung. Those who worship idols and images as gods, pray in vain to inane phantoms, but those who esteem and follow the Scriptures know the origin of everything. The Holy Scriptures and the eternal wisdom supply and complete each other to state and conform wherefrom and how man was created. All confessors of this creed strive after good deeds, fulfil it, and abhor sin."

## II.

### The Memorial Stone of 1488 C.E.

"Abraham the patriarch who founded the Israelitish religion, was the nineteenth *) descendant from Adam. From the beginning of the world, the patriarchs have handed down the precept, that we must not make images and similitudes, and that we must not worship superior and inferior spirits; for neither can images and similitudes protect, nor superior and inferior spirits afford us aid. The patriarch thinking upon Heaven, the pure and ethereal Being who dwells in high, the most honourable and without compose, that Divine providence, who, without speaking, causes the four seasons to revolve and the myriad of things to grow; and looking at the budding of spring, the growth of summer, the ingathering of the harvest, and the storing of winter,—at the objects that fly, dive, move and vegetate, whether they flourish or decay, bloom or droop, all so easy and natural in their productions and transformations, in their assumptions of form and colour, was suddenly roused to reflection, and understood this deep mystery; he then sincerely sought after the correct instruction, and adoringly praised the

---

*) It is to be accounted for by the omission of Cainan from the genealogy.

true Heaven; with his whole heart he served, and with undivided attention reverenced Him ; by this means he set up the foundation of religion, and caused it to be handed down to the present day. This happened according to our inquiry in the 146th year of the Chow state. From him the doctrines were handed down to the great teacher and legislator Moses, who according to our computation lived about the 613th year of the same state.*) This man was intelligent from his birth, pure and disinterested, endowed with benevolence and righteousness, virtue and wisdom all complete; he sought and obtained the sacred writings on the top of Sinai's Hill, where he fasted forty days and nights, repressing his carnal desires, refraining even from sleep, and spending his time in sincere devotion. His piety moved the heart of Heaven and the sacred

---

\*) We can not refer this to the Chow dynasty, which commenced B.C. 1122, the 146th year of which would synochronize with the time of Rehabom ; and no Israelite could be so ignorant of the antiquity of his race, as to suppose that Abraham flourished only 1000 years B.C. We are necessitated therefore to refer the Chow spoken of in the text, to the state founded by Han-tsi, who flourished in the days of Shun B.C. 2254; between which date and that of B.C. 1766 when the Shang state was consolidated we must look for the period from which the 146 years referring to Abraham, and the 613 years referring to Moses, is to be reckoned.

writings, amounting to 53 sections *) were thus obtained. Their contents are deep and mysterious, their promises calculated to influence men's good feelings, and their threatenings to repress their corrupt imaginations. The doctrines were again handed down to the time of the reformer of religion and wise instructor Ezra, whose descent was reckoned from the founder of our religion, and whose teaching contained the right clue to his instructions, viz.: the duty of honouring Heaven by appropriate worship; so that he could be considered capable of unfolding the mysteries of the religion of our forefathers.

But religion must consist in the purity and truth of Divine worship. Purity refers to the pure One, who is without mixture; truth to the correct One, who is without corruption; worship consists in reverence and in bowing down to the ground. Men in their daily avocations must not for a single moment forget Heaven, but at the hours of four in the morning, mid-day, and six in

---

*) The Pentateuch is divided in our Common Bibles in 54 sections, but in Pentateuchs brought from Persia, the Massoretic 52nd and 53rd sections are combined in one, making together 53 sections. Seemingly, the division in 53 sections aims at giving one section for every Sabbath of the 52 Sabbaths of the year, and the last section (Deut. 33-34) for Shemini Atzereth or Simchath Torah.

the evening, should thrice perform their adorations, which is the true principle of the religion of Heaven. The form observed by the virtuous men of antiquity was first to bathe and wash their heads, taking care at the same time to purify their hearts and correct their senses, after which they reverently approached before Eternal Reason and the sacred writings. Eternal Reason is without form or figure, like the Eternal Reason of Heaven, exalted on high. We will here endeavour to set forth the general course of Divine worship in order. First, the worshipper bending his body, does reverence to Eternal Reason, by which means he recognizes Eternal Reason as present in such bending of the body; then standing upright in the midst, without declining, he does obeisance to Eternal Reason, by which means he recognizes Eternal Reason as standing in the midst; in stillness, maintaining his spirit and silently praising, he venerates Eternal Reason showing that he incessantly remembers Heaven, in motion, examining himself and lifting up his voice, he honours Eternal Reason, showing that he unfailingly remembers Heaven. This is the way in which our religion teaches us to look towards invisible space and perform our adorations. Retiring three paces, the worshipper gets suddenly to the rear, to show his reverence for the Eternal Reason who is behind him, advancing five steps he looks on before, to show his reverence for the Eternal Reason, who is in front of his person, he bows towards the left, reverencing Eternal Reason whereby he admires the Eternal Reason, who is on his left; he bows towards the right, reverencing Eternal Reason, whereby he adores the Eternal Reason who is on his right; looking up he reverences Eternal Reason, to show that he considers Eternal Reason as above him; looking down, he reverences Eternal Reason, to show that he considers Eternal Reason as close to him; at the close he worships Eternal Reason manifesting reverence in his act of adoration. But to venerable Heaven and to neglect ancestors is to fail in the services which are their due. In the spring and autumn, therefore, men sacrifice to their ancestors, to show that they serve the dead as they do the living, and pay the same respect to the departed that they do to those who survive, they offer sheep and oxen, and present the fruits of the season, to show that they do not neglect the honour due to ancestors, when they are gone from us. During the course of every month we fast and abstain four times, which constitutes the door by which religion is entered, and the basis of which goodness is accumulated. It is called an entrance, because we practice one act of goodness to-day, and another to-morrow; thus having commenced the merit of abstinence, we add to our store, avoiding the practice of every vice, and reverently performing every virtue. Every seventh day we observe a holy rest, which when terminated begins anew; as it is said in the Tih-king. *)

The good man in the practice of virtue, apprehends lest the time should prove too short. At each of the four seasons, we lay ourselves under a seven days restraint, in remembrance of the trials endured by our ancestors; by which means, we venerate our predecessors and reward our progenitors; we also abstain entirely from food during a whole day, when we reverently pray to Heaven, repent of our former faults, and practice anew the duties of each day. The Tih-king also says: "When the wind and thunder prevail, the good man thinks of what virtues he

---

\*) The Tih-king (Book of Permutations) is one of the sacred writings of the Chinese. According to tradition it was composed in the time of Noah, when Emperor Fu-hi reigned in China (2850 B.C.E.). Another version says that the Book has been delivered from Heaven to Emperor Fu-hi.

The Book is thoroughly mystic and esoteric, and it very much resembles the Jewish Cabbalistic "Sepher Jetzirah."

In my Hebrew book on China and on the Jews in China ("Hassinim" London 1911) I adduced many parallels of these two mystic books.

shall practice, and if he has any errors, he reforms them."

Thus our religion system has been handed down and communicated from one to another. It came originally from Teen-chu (India). Those who introduced it in obedience to the Divine commands were seventy Tsungs (clans) viz: those of Yen, Li, Ngai, Kau, Muh, Chaw, Kin, Chao, Chang, Shih, Hwang, Nieh, Tso, Pih, etc. These brought as tribute some Western cloth. The Emperor of the Sung dynasty *) said "Since they have come to our central Land, and reverently observe the cutsoms of their ancestors, let them hand down their doctrines at Pien-Lang (now Kai-fung-fu)" In the year 1163 C.E. Lieh Ching and Wu-sz-ta superintended this religion, and Yen-tu-lah built the Synagogue. In the year 1279 C.E. Wu-sz-ta rebuilt the ancient Temple of Truth and Purity, which was situated in the Tu-shi-tze street, on the south-east side; on each side the area of the Temple extended 350 feet.

When the first Emperor of the Ming dynasty established his throne and pacified the people of the Empire (1390 C.E.), all those who came under the civilizing influence of our country were presented with ground, on which they might

---

*) Probably the Northern Sung which flourished 519 C.E.

dwell quietly, and profess their religion without molestation, in order to manifest a feeling of sympathizing benevolence, which views all alike. But as this Temple required someone to look after its concerns, there were appointed for that purpose Li-ching, Li-Shih, Yen-Ping-tu, Ngai King, Chow, Ngan, Li-king, etc., who were themselves upright and intelligent men, and able to admonish others, having attained the title of Manlah. So that up to this time, the sacred vestments, ceremonies and music, are all maintained according to the prescribed pattern, and every word and action is conformed to the ancient rule, every man therefore keeps the laws, and knows how to reverence Heaven and respect the patriarchs, being faithful to the prince and filial to parents, all in consequence of the efforts of these teachers.

Yen-Ching, who was skilled in medicine, in the year 1421 C.E. received the imperial commands communicated through Chau-fuh Ting Wang, to present incense in the Temple of Truth and Purity, which was then repaired; about the same time also, there was received the imperial tablet of the Ming dynasty to be erected in the temple. In the year 1422 C.E. the above-named officer reported, that he had executed some trust reposed in him; whereupon the Emperor changed his surname to Chau, and conferred upon him an embroidered garment, and a title of dignity elevating him to be a magistrate in Cheh-kiang province. In the year 1446, Li-yung and some others built the three rooms in front of the synagogue.

It appears that in the fourth year of the Emperor King-ti (1461 C.E.) the Yellow River had inundated the synagogue, but the foundations were still preserved; whereupon Ngai-king and others petitioned to be allowed to restore it to its original form, and through the chief magistrate of the prefecture, received an order from the Treasurer of the Honan Province, granting that it might be done in conformity with the old form of the Temple of Truth and Purity that had existed in the time of Chi-Yuen (1290 C.E.), whereupon Li-Yung provided the funds, and the whole was made quite new.

During the reign of Ching-hwa (1470 C.E.) Kaw-Kien provided the funds for repairing three rooms at the back of the synagogue. He also deposited therein three volumes of the sacred writings. Such is the history of the front and back rooms of the synagogue. During the reign of Tien-Shun (1450 C.E.) Shih-Pin, Kau-Kien, and Chang-Hiuen, had brought from the professors of this religion at Ning-po, one volume of the sacred writings; while Chan-Ying-Ching, of Ningpo, sent another volume of the Divine word, which was presented to the synagogue at Pienlang (Kai-fung-fu). His younger brother Ying also provided funds, and in the second year of Hung chi (1488) strengthened the foundations of the synagogue. Ying with myself, Chung, entrusted to Chau-Tsun the setting up of the present tablet: Yen-tu-lah had already fixed the foundation of the building, and commenced the work, towards the completion of which all the families contributed, and thus provided the sacred implements and furniture connected with the cells for depositing the sacred writings, causing the whole synagogue to be painted and ornamented, and put in a state of complete repair. For I conceive that the three religions of China have each their respective Temples, and severally honour the founders of their faith; among the literati, there is the Temple of Ta-ching (Great Perfection), dedicated to Confucius; among the Buddhists, there is the Temple of Shing-yung (the Sacred Countenance), dedicated to Niman (Buddha); and among the Taoists, there is the Temple of Yuh-hwang. So also in the True and Pure religion there is the Temple of Israel, erected to the honour of Hwang-tien (the Great Heaven). Although our religion agrees in many respects with the religion of the literati, from which it differs in a slight degree, yet the main design of it is nothing more than reverence for Heaven, and veneration for ancestors, fidelity to the prince, and obedience to parents, just that which is included in the five human relations, the five constant virtues, with the three principal connections of life. It is to be observed, however, that people merely know that in the Temple of Truth and Purity ceremonies are performed, when we reverence Heaven, and worship towards no visible object; but they do not know that the great origin of Eternal Reason comes from Heaven, and that what has been handed down from the old to the present day, must not be falsified.

Although our religion enjoins worship thus earnestly, we do not render it merely with the view of securing happiness to ourselves, but seeing that we have received the favours of the prince, and enjoyed the emoluments conferred by him, we carry to the utmost our sincerity in worship with the view of manifesting fidelity to our prince, and gratitude to our country. Thus we pray that the Emperor's rule may be extended to myriads of years, and the Imperial dynasty may be firmly established; as long as heaven and earth endure, may there be favourable winds and seasonable showers, with the mutual enjoyment of tranquility. We have engraven these our ideas on the imperishable marble, that they may be handed down to the latest generation.

Composed by a promoted literary graduate of the prefecture of Kai-fung-fu, named Kin-Chung; inscribed by a literary graduate of purchased rank belonging to the district Tsiang-fu, named Tsau-Tso; and engraven by a literary graduate of purchased rank, belonging to the prefecture of Kai-fung-fu, named Fu-Ju. Erected on a fortunate day, in the middle of summer, in the second year of Hung-Chi (1488 C.E.), by a disciple of the religion of Truth and Purity.

### III.

#### The Memorial Stone of 1151 C.E.

It has been said that the sacred writings are for the purpose of embodying Eternal Reason, and that Eternal Reason is for the purpose of communicating the sacred writings. What is Eternal Reason? The principle which is in daily use and constant practice; and which has been generally followed out by men of ancient and modern times. It is present in everything, and the same in all seasons; in fact there is no place in which Eternal Reason does not reside. But

Eternal Reason without the sacred writings cannot be preserved; and the sacred writings without Eternal Reason cannot be carried out into action; for men get into confusion, and do not know whither they are going, until they are carried away by foolish schemes and strange devices; hence the doctrines of the Sages have been handed down in the six sacred classics*) in order to convey the knowledge to future generations, and to extend his benefits to the most distant period.

With respect to the Israelitish religion, we find on inquiry, that its first ancestor Adam came originally from Teen-chu (India) and during the Chow state the sacred writings were in existence. The sacred writings embodying Eternal Reason consist of 53 sections. The principles therein contained are very obstruse, and the Eternal Reason therein revealed is very mysterious, being treated with the same veneration as Heaven. The founder of this religion is Abraham, who is considered the first teacher of it. Then came Moses. who established the law, and handed down the sacred writings. After his time, during the Han dynasty this religion entered

---

*) The sacred classics of the Chinese: 1. Yih-king. 2. Shi-king. 3. Shu-king. 4. Li-king. 5. Chin-Chiu, and 6. Lun-yu, leaving unmentioned the sacred writings which were composed and compiled after Confucius.

China. In 1164 C.E. a synagogue was built at Pien (Kai-fung-fu). In 1296 C.E. the old Temple was rebuilt, as a place in which the sacred writings might be deposited with veneration.

Those who practice this religion are to be found in other places besides Pien (Kai-fung-fu) but wherever they are met with, throughout the whole world, they all without exception honour the sacred writings, and venerate Eternal Reason. The characters in which the sacred writings are penned, differ indeed from those employed in the books of the learned in China, but if we trace their principles up to their origin, we shall find that they are originally none other than the Eternal Reason which is commonly followed by mankind. Hence it is that when Eternal Reason is followed by rulers and subjects, rules will be respectful, and subjects faithful; when Eternal Reason is followed by parents and children, parents will be kind, and children filial; when Eternal Reason is followed by elder and younger brothers, the former will be friendly and the latter reverential; when Eternal Reason is followed by husbands and wives, husbands will be harmonious, and wives obedient; when Eternal Reason is followed by friends and companions, then they will severally become faithful and sincere. In Eternal Reason there is nothing greater than benevolence and rectitude, and in following it out, men naturally display the feeling of compassion and a sense of shame; in Eternal Reason there is nothing greater than propriety and wisdom, and in following it out, men naturally exhibit the feeling of respect and a sense of rectitude. When Eternal Reason is followed in fasting and abstinence, men necessarily feel reverential and awe-struck; when Eternal Reason is followed out in sacrificing to ancestors, men necessarily feel filial and sincere; when Eternal Reason is followed in Divine worship, men bless and praise high Heaven, the Producer and Nourisher of the myriad of things, while in their demeanour and carriage they consider sincerity and respect as the one thing needful. With respect to widows and orphans, the poor and the destitute, together with the sick and maimed, the deaf and dumb, these must all be relieved and assisted, that they may not utterly fail. When poor men wish to marry and have not the means, or when such wish to inter-relative, and are not able to accomplish it, the necessary expenses for such must be duly provided. Only let those who are mourning for their friends carefully avoid rich viands and intoxicating liquors, and those who are conducting funeral ceremonies not be emulous of external pomp. Let them in the first place avoid complying with superstitious customs, and in the second place, not make molten or graven images, but in everything follow the ceremonies that have been introduced from Teen-chu. Let there be no false weights and measures employed in trade, with the view of defrauding others.

Looking around us on the professors of this religion, we find that there are some who strive for literary honours, aiming to exalt their parents and distinguish themselves; there are some who engage in government employ both at Court and in the provinces, seeking to serve their prince and benefit the people, while some defend the country and resist the enemy, thus displaying their pattriotism by their faithful conduct; there are others again, who in private stations cultivate personal virtue, and diffuse their influence over a whole region; others there are who plough the waste land, sustaining their share of the public burdens; and others who attend to mechanical arts, doing their part towards supporting the state; or who follow mercantile pursuits, and thus gather in profit from every quarter: but all of them should venerate the command of Heaven, obey the royal laws, attend to the five constant virtues, observe the duties of the human relations, reverently follow the customs of their ancestors, be filial towards their parents, respectful to their superiors, harmonious among their neighbours, and friendly with their associates, teaching their children and descendants, thus laying up a store of good works, while they repress trifling animosities, in order to complete great affairs; the main idea of all the prohibitions and commands consists in standing to those things. This in fact is the great object set forth in the sacred writings, and the daily and constant duties inculcated by Eternal Reason. Thus the command of Heaven influencing virtuous nature, is by this means carried out to perfection; the religion which inculcates obedience to Eternal Reason is by this means entered upon; and the virtues of benevolence, rectitude, propriety, and wisdom are by this means maintained.

From the beginning of the world our first father Adam handed the doctrine down to Abraham, Abraham handed it down to Isaac, Isaac handed it down to Jacob, Jacob handed it down to the twelve patriarchs and the twelve patriarchs handed it down to Moses; Moses handed it down to Aaron, Aaron handed it down to Joshua and Joshua handed it down to Ezra, by whom the doctrines of the holy religion were first sent abroad, and the letters of the Jewish nation first made plain. All those who profess this religion aim at the practice of goodness, and avoid the commission of vice, morning and evening performing their devotion, and with a sincere mind cultivating personal virtues

They practice fasting and abstinence on the prescribed days, and bring eating and drinking under proper regulations. They make the sacred writings their study and their rule, obeying and believing them in every particular; then may they expect that the blessing of Heaven will abundantly, and the favour of providence be unfailingly conferred; every individual obtaining the credit of virtuous conduct, and every family experiencing the happiness of Divine protection. In this way perhaps our professors will not fail of carrying out the religion handed down by their ancestors, nor will they neglect the ceremonies which they are bound to observe.

We have engraved this on a tablet, placed in the synagogue, to be handed down to distant ages, that future generations may carefully consider it.

This tablet was erected by the families Tou-Tang, Yen, Li, Kau, Chau, Kin, J, and Chang, at the rebuilding of the synagogue, in the first month of autumn, in the 7th year of Emperor Ching-teh of the Ming dynasty (1511 C.E.).

## IV.

### The Memorial Stone of 1663 C.E.

The composer of the inscription begins with an abundance of prefatory phrases to make it clear that there is nothing in the sacred writings of the Jews which does not tally with the six sacred writings of the Chinese. He exerts himself to inculcate it as an axiomatic certitude. He praises the constancy of the Jews in religious matters, and adds that the Chinese scarcely differ from them in the worship of heaven, in the duties of civil life and in honouring the dead. He also gives details of the history of the Jews in China in nearly the same words as the memorial stone of 1488. He relates of the sorrows and misfortunes which have afflicted the Jews in 1642 C.E., the year when the Ming dynasty was deposed, and Kai-fung-fu was besieged for 6 months by the rebel Li-tse-tsing. He describes at length the inundation of the town which was caused by order of the commander of the Emperor's forces to destroy the dikes of the Yellow River with the purpose of flooding the town and drowning the rebels. It relates that a great number of Jews lost their lives, and only some 200 families, who escaped over the river northsides saved their lives, and that the synagogue was destroyed, and 26 of the sacred volumes were lost. The inscription mentions also the names of those people who did not shrink from waging their lives in rescuing the sacred volumes from the floods. It relates that these sacred books which were saved from the waves, and other books which were recovered from the rubbish-heaps among ruins, were brought into the house of a private man outside the town, where the Jews used to assemble for prayers.

Ten years afterwards—the inscription continues—a Jewish Mandarin Tsao-ying-tseng, visited the place with a detachment of soldiers who served under his command. They rebuilt the town, repaired the roads, restored the bridges and helped the sufferers. Great assistance has been given to Tsao-ying-tseng by his brother Ying-te, and they succeeded in settling the poor Jews in the neighbourhood of the synagogue, which was rebuilt in the 10th year of the Emperor Shin-chi (1653 C.E.), who was the first Emperor of the Ta-tsing (the Mandsu) dynasty.

The inscription gives many details in describing the case taken by the learned Jews to revise, restore and transcribe the sacred books, and mentions the names of seven families who chiefly occupied themselves with the task, and provided the largest part of the necesssary funds. It relates also that from all the Thorah-rolls which were rescued from the floods in a damaged condition only one could be made complete, and they put this one Thorah-roll, with great devotion, in a shrine purposely constructed for it. In the same shrine they also put, with no less veneration, twelve more Thorah-rolls which they succeeded to acquire with great efforts. A centre was created once more, and the Jews gathered around it and united themselves, forming a new congregation.

Before Tsao-ying-tseng left the town he noted down in a book all the particulars of the said incidents, and his brother Ying-te edited a book of ten chapters recording in it all the abovementioned events. He records that there were many Jewish Mandarins who helped in every direction to bring about the re-erection of the synagogue, and to put up the memorial stone for imparting all these occurrences to the later generations. This inscription has been engraved in the second year of Emperor Kang-hi of the Tatsing (Mandsu) dynasty (1663 C,E.).

❋ ❋ ❋

When we carefully examine the inscriptions above produced, it cannot escape our attention that the composers of them were animated by quite a different spirit, and the inferences will lead us to the conclusion that in the 500 years which passed between 1164 to 1663 the process of absorption has gradually worked upon the Jews in China till they were doomed completely.

The inscription of 1164 distinguishes itself by very proud and haughty phrases, accentuating the superiority of the Jews, over those who "worship idols and images as gods" as they "pray in vain to inane phantoms, but those who esteem and follow the scriptures know the origin of everything," from which it is obvious that the Jews had taken umbrage at the religions of China, resenting their monotheism as not being pure, because of the images they adored. Not such a spirit prevails in the inscriptions which were composed three hundred years after. The tone of the inscriptions of 1488 and 1511 is quite a different one, as the Jews, certainly have then been to a great degree absorbed by the Chinese, and so they were contented to defend their position by extolling their religion as a true and pure one, to praise their patriarchs and lawgivers, but they did not offend or attack the Chinese religions. There is no more an allusion to idolatory of other creeds, moreover we see that they had already adopted from the Chinese some customs of piety and ceremonies, being ignorant of the fact that they were in disharmony with Jewish religious precepts, e g the sacrifices to dead ancestors, the burning of incense in the Temple, and above all the references constantly made to the Yih-king and other sacred books of the Chinese, and as a corollary to it the translation of "Jahveh" by "Tao" (according to Alexei Winogradoff).

Some 150 years later, when the absorption was nearly completed, and there was no hope left, they did not struggle any more, they resigned and sought only to vindicate their deeds in the inscription of 1663 which they left behind them, wording it to the effect, that the Jewish and Chinese religions did not contradict each other, but were at one, in all and everything. The drift of this last inscription is rather of a defending character, aiming to palliate the assimilation, and to soften the accomplished fact of having been merged into the Chinese nation.

❋ ❋

Before declaring my opinion on the circumstances which decided the fate of the Jews in China, I have to premise that all the Jewish settlements were undubitably situated in the provinces bordering on the Yellow River, that most destructive stream on the face of the earth, which has been named the "Sorrow of China," and that the Yellow River has repeatedly devastated the land by overflowing and made havoc in the settlements of the Jews. When such a disaster befell the inhabitants of the shores, some of the well-to-do Jews emigrated to other provinces, and to them the record on the memorial stone of 1511 refers, saying "Those who practice this religion are to be found in other places besides Pen." The emigrants, few in number as they were, and being scattered over different provinces away from their co-religionists, have soon been isolated, and when absorbed by the Chinese left no trace at all.

\* \* \*

Two forces combined worked simultaneously towards the doom of the Jews in China, one of them being of a physical character, and the other of a purely spiritual one. By the physical force I mean the overwhelming majority of the native people, which, in case of being not of a lower cultural standing than the alien minority, and if in intercourse with the foreigner treats him kindly, not making him feel to be a stranger, must in course of time, by quite a natural process grind the minority, crumble off parts of them and gradually absorb them. This normal process, which acted upon the Jews in China has been considerably accelerated by inundations and revolutions which time after time decimated them and lessened their power of resistance. By the spiritual force I understand the high ethical and philosophical standing of the religions of China at that time, which—as I have already mentioned in Part I.—caused the Jews to abdicate their superiority, to take up Chinese learning, and to assimilate to and mingle with the dominant majority.

\* \* \*

The decline of the Jewish nation had commenced when the kingdom of Israel was subverted by Shalmaneser, and the ten—now lost—tribes were banished at Assyria and Media (721 B.C.E.) But still the kingdom of Judah existed, although tributary to the King of Assyria (II Kings 18. 14-16) and was so powerless and few in number that the Prophet Isaiah designated them as "a remnant that is escaped of the house of Judah" (II Kings 19. 30). They must have been so few and so dreadfully incapacious to be even unfit to be a physical medium for consummating a miracle through them; the Jews were no more considered apt enough to meet the Assyrian army on the battlefield, to combat and vanquish it, but an Angel of the Lord had to come and smite it (II Kings 19. 35) yet they were still a nation settled on their own land with a King of their own brethren reigning over them.

But it was quite natural that this weak nation surrounded by enemies should fall, and the second deciding blow hit them by the destruction of the first Temple by Nebuchadnezzar (588 B.C.E.) when the Jews were exiled at Babylon. Since that time the Jews have no more recovered, they never recuperated vitality enough to rise and consolidate into a great nation. The return of the Jews to Jerusalem at the time of Zerubbabel and Ezra (531 and 458 B.C.E. resp.) and the organised commonwealth was only a faint reflex of the glory which had passed away not to return.

But although during the long time of the existence of the commonwealth, when the Jewish land had been a bone of contest for many kings thirsting for conquest, the Jews were hindered from regaining their secular independeucy and from rising and elevating spiritually, *) still they were concentrated on their territory and could be called a nation. They did not despair, they even revived occasionally and inspired some selected plucky individuals and produced even heroes, such as the Maccabeans have been.

The Jews being under the sway of Roman procurators and besides it harassed by constant domestic intrigues and quarrels for gaining profitable and influential positions, debased constantly, and simony and nepotism was rife and rampant, so much so that even the rank and office of the High-priest became a negotiable object, and was often purchased by rich and powerful ignorant villains. In everything it went from bad

---

*) משמתו נביאים הראשונים בטלו אורים וטומים (סוטה מ"ח א')
After the demise of the first Prophets the Urim W'thumim have ceased to work.

משמתו נביאים האחרונים, הגי זכריה ומלאכי, נסתלקה רוח הקדש מישראל (כנהדרין י"א א.)
After the death of the last Prophets, Haggai, Zechariah and Malachi, the Holy Spirit of prophecy has departed from the Jews.

אלו חמשה דברים שהיו בין קדש ראשון למקדש שני ואלו הן:
ארון וכפורת וכרובים, אש, ושכינה, ורוח הקדש, ואורים ותמים
(יומא כ"א ב.).
Among the five preferences which the first Temple has had over the second, there are mentioned "the Holy Ghost of God, the Holy Spirit of prophecy and the Urim W'thumim.

to worse, and especially after the death of Herodes, who, when wielding the power invested upon him, was strong and ambitious enough to maintain his prestige. The condition became unbearable and untenable, both through the exhorbitant extortions of the rapacious and venal Roman functionaries and by the Jewish domineering oppressors; the people revolted repeatedly and the unavoidable consequence was the total suppression of the revolution, and the destruction of the Temple, the annihilation of the commonwealth and the diaspora.

This was the end of the Jewish nation! The insurrections attempted afterwards are not worth mentioning, as they were only convulsions of a dying body.

\* \* \*

The Jews have then been dispersed all over the world, and since that time they have been constantly under the same twofold influence which worked upon the off-shoots of those of our brethren who took refuge in China, and on whom this influence turned out to be so strong as to cause the withering of that branch of our nation. The Jews were now everywhere a small minority, and came face to face with alien cultures.

Though I have already expressed in Part I my opinion, why the Chinese succeeded in absorbing the Jews, whereas neither the Christians nor the Mohammedans can boast of such a result, yet I consider it as essential to treat the question more fully, with the special view to make use of the inferences which we may draw from investigating more closely into the causes, which brought about the success of the first-mentioned country and the failure of the others.

In analysing the accessory circumstances of that enigma of the unlike results, we will soon detect many discriminating points, proving that only superficially the causes seem to be homogenous, but not similar in intrinsical worthiness. It is true that in both cases, in the diaspora as in China, the Jews have been a small minority, among a great majority of the dominant natives, and even their numbers have been diminished in Christian and Mohammedan countries by persecutions and molestations as in China by inundations and revolutions. It is also true that the Jews came into the diaspora under the influence of alien cultures as it was the case in China. But the main difference lies therein, that whereas in China the dominant majority attracted the immigrated Jews by amicably approaching them, had the persecutions and oppressions developed strong repulsive feelings among the Jews, and so the influence which the majority should have had on the minority was paralysed, and the Jewish minority took up a strong defending attitude and fortified their positions. It is obvious that the diminution of the Jewish population which had accelerated the absorption of the Jews in China, had produced the quite contrary result in the diaspora. The second influence, the spiritual one had been still more invalid, because at that time the culture in general was based solely on theological knowledge of a pugnacious tendency, and as the weapons of both combating parties, of the Christians or Mohammedans and of the Jews had to be borrowed mostly from the Jewish arsenal, the holy scriptures, on which they all relied, the Jews felt themselves stronger and superior to their combatants and remained invulnerable and impregnable. Not so has been the case in China, where the dominant nation had their own sacred writings which had not the slightest reference to the Jewish scriptures, and the Chinese did not assault the Jewish religion, but made their genuine culture work smoothly, gently and slowly upon the Jews; they did not fight the Jews but attracted them till they found themselves unawares transformed into Chinese.

The Jewish nation is at the present time once

more in a very critical position, and the influences of the decomposing forces are now, more than ever, menacing to destroy them, and more dangerous because of the altered intrinsic value of the forces which are busy to exterminate them.

The times, when the cultural weapons against the Jews were solely theological ones, are gone for ever, the religions are not considered any more to be the fountains of learning and knowledge, not even is it now regarded as an object of great importance—it has become a quantite negligeable. Nation after nation strives to check the influence of religion by separating state and church, and by excluding religion from the schools. The dignity and influence of religion in bygone times will be inherited by science which will occupy the foremost place in the ethical and spiritual world, and in cases of contradiction between the teachings of science and the teachings of the scriptures nobody will exert any more to force harmonious meanings into them, but ignore the scriptural teachings and take the teachings of science as indisputable truths.

On this battlefield, the battlefield of science, the Jews not only have never been at the fore but have always had to borrow from the Gentiles, hence the danger that the Jews will nolens volens have to give in and become assimilated. We cannot gainsay the fact that all our prominent men of practical and scientific standing have been brought up on secular education, which has nothing to do with Jewish learning, and the culture with which they were imbued has already worked upon them so much as to estrange from us a great many of our best intellectual men, of whom a certain percentage even abandoned us altogether and merged into the majority.

At the present critical and most perilous juncture a reaction has set in, and we are witnesses of a strong movement towards resurrection, which has attracted and revived not only the great masses, who are destined to provide for the rank and file of the combatants and of the restorers of the nation, but even many of those who were since long staying aside from their brethren, have given testimony of their readiness to return to their nation, to unite with those whom they have forsaken, and have declared to share their lot, and to assist them as far as it will be in their power.

We must confess that the initiative to the movement did not come from a spontaneous impulse of the Jews themselves, but was called forth by accidents from without; it was the outcry of the suffering Jews which awakened the slumbering consciences, e.g. the terrible injustice which was committed by France in 1894 against the innocent Captain Dreyfus, the vehicle to bring back to his brethren the half and half assimilated Dr. Theodor Herzl, who, in his capacity as correspondent for the Neue Freie Presse was present at the degradation of Dreyfus. The horrible oppressions of the Jews in Roumania, the barbaric persecutions and pogroms of the Jews in Russia evoked the protests of the enlightened West, and stirred up all those Jews who were living in peace among cultured peoples and had forgotten their hapless brethren. But the fact that the movement has come through our enemies does not debase the regeneration which they brought about. Has not Moses himself been stimulated by the occurrence "that he went out unto his brethren, and looked on their burdens" (Exod.2.11), and does not Nehemiah record that he was spurned to act because Hanani related to him that "the remnant that are left of the captivity there in the province are in great affliction and reproach" (Nehemiah 1. 3)?

The movement is strenuously acting all over the world where Jews are living, all, or nearly all of them are animated with the stern desire to bring deliverance to the nation, and to erect once more the house of Israel. And I do not hesitate to aver that—should our people act in perfect harmony, all aiming at one goal—we would, without the slightest doubt, succeed, and our endeavours would be brought to perfection to our satisfaction. And when we will succeed so far as to get a territory on autonomic principles granted and guaranteed by one of the enlightened great powers, we could—there is no doubt of it—develop into a vital and prosperous nation to the profit of ourselves and of the great power, to the suzerainity of which we will always be faithful vassals. I even contend that the conditions for success are more favourable at the present time than even at the time of Zerubbabel and Ezra, when the Jews returned to Jerusalem by the grace of the Kings of Persia. The political conditions of the world are in general more stable and more regulated than they have been some 2500 years ago.

That our nation, in case that all forces should unite together could command an abundance of talented men, sufficient to provide every governmental department with a strenuous staff of officers, nobody will gainsay. Only we must not split our strength on problems of no importance e.g. we ought not to lay stress on things of a minor value like the question: in which particular part of the world the territory of refuge *must* be situated, in Asia, Africa or America, as if it make an essential difference on which geographical spot of the globe it will be, as if it were not sufficient when the territory will be of a healthy climate, and of a fertile soil, and all other economical conditions will be favourable to the settlement of a nation. The main thing, as a *conditio sine qua non* is that all of us shall work in harmony without taking the slightest private interest in consideration.

We will also have to pay due attention to the requirements of the spirit of the age. It is self-evident that it would not do to make use of such like means for instance as those applied by Nehemiah, who records "And I contended with them, and cursed them, and smote certain of them, and plucked off their hair, and made them swear by God, saying, "Ye shall not give your daughters unto their sons, nor take their daughters unto your sons, or for yourselves" (Nehemiah 13.25) In our time, I dare say, other persuasive means would be more suitable and more effective. And certainly there would be a strong opposition, and it would provoke quarrels and hatred, should we decide to take the deeds of Ezra and Nehemiah as samples and act accordingly. I refer to the command to turn out, both, the wives they had married long before and their children they bore them, as it is written in Ezra chap. 10, or to drive away the son of the high priest because he happened to be the son-in-law of Sanballat (Nehemiah 13. 28). Such like vigorous means certainly would cause a rupture of the nation, and bring about the exodus of the more tolerant and liberal Jews from the rank and file of the nation.

The only straight way for our nation is to acquire a territory to concentrate the bulk of the nation there, which will form the dominant majority of the country. Such a country will become a place where genuine Jewish culture, and the cultures of other nations will influence each other and fuse together, and the composition would give birth to new culture, the shape of which it is impossible to define yet. But surely this new culture, which will contain a certain portion of Jewish culture, although many parts of its contents will be gleaned from the cultures of other nations, will be entitled to name itself "Jewish culture" because of having been developed by the Jewish nation in the Jewish territory Of the profits it will gain from the foreign ethics, we may say, applying the words of the Talmudists „יפאתו של יפת באהלי שם" (מגילה ט') "Those excellent learnings of Japhet will be taught in the tents of Shem" I understand it to mean at the time when the Jews will possess *their own tents, their own homes, in their own land.*

We must be candid and not bring ourselves into a state of hypnosis by auto suggestions, and it is of no avail to deny the historical facts, that whensoever a minority comes under the strong influence of a cultured majority, and if the majority does not repulse the minority, the majority absorbs it. We need not look for testimonies into the histories of other nations, as we ourselves have had enough experiences: we have seen that the Jews have nearly been absorbed in free countries like Italy and France, we have seen that the Jews have become totally extinct in China; we must not be blind to the fact that the repressive measures in Russia and Roumania, and the sham emancipation in Germany and Austria, was the only pressing power from without to keep the Jews together and unite them, in order to defend themselves as much as possible. And therefore the danger is not imminent in those countries where the hostility to the Jews is still strong and effective, because they will fight there and conserve themselves. But we have to look forward, to the time which must come sooner or later, to the time when the Jews will enjoy the same privileges as the dominant people, as the Germans, the Roumanians and the Russians, Then the process of grinding and annihilating of the minority will commence all over the world and work rapidly, because there will be heard no more groans of any oppressed to remind the Jews that they were once a strong nation, and are about to be destroyed from the face of the earth. Therefore we have to look out for means to prevent the process of absorption, and *the only remedy is, as I have said, a territory for the Jews.*

Let us not lull our conscience, and deceive ourselves with empty phantoms, e.g. such as that the numerous Jewish immigrants in America will restore and consolidate the Jews as a nation; to comfort us with such-like hopes is self-delusion, because it is contrary to the laws of natural development. The revival called forth by the numerous Jewish immigrants in America will be only a temporary one, and the shortsighted optimists alone may rejoice at such a regeneration and be satisfied with it. The Jewish immigrants could restore the nation if they were all in one state of the United States, forming there a majority, but being in the cities and commercial centres they will be able only to check the process of absorption for some time, say for a hundred or two hundred years, but will not be strong enough to paralyze it for ever. There is no more a possibility of retaining a scattered minority to form a compact nation, as it is unthinkable to rely exclusively on crops nursed in hothouses for steadily providing food for the population of a whole country. We have seen that the process of absorption of the Jews in China has taken five hundred years, a long time it was, still they have finally been swallowed up by the Chinese; and some hundred or two hundred years are a short time for an old nation as we are.

So long the Jews will be scattered among a majority with a scientific culture—and it will not be a long time till all nations will have scientific cultures—the majority must by degrees increase their influence and become the absolute masters of the intellects of all, and the Jews must and will merge into it.

I will conclude by repeating once more that we need a territory, and to acquire it we need a harmonious action of all our forces, the intellectual and physical combined. But it is not an easy task to complete such an achievement, and it requires a strong organisation and a brisk propaganda, to awaken the interest of the influential men among us. I dare not make proposals how to bring about the organisation and the propaganda, and I will not obtrude myself as an uncalled for adviser, moreover this book is not the proper place for it.

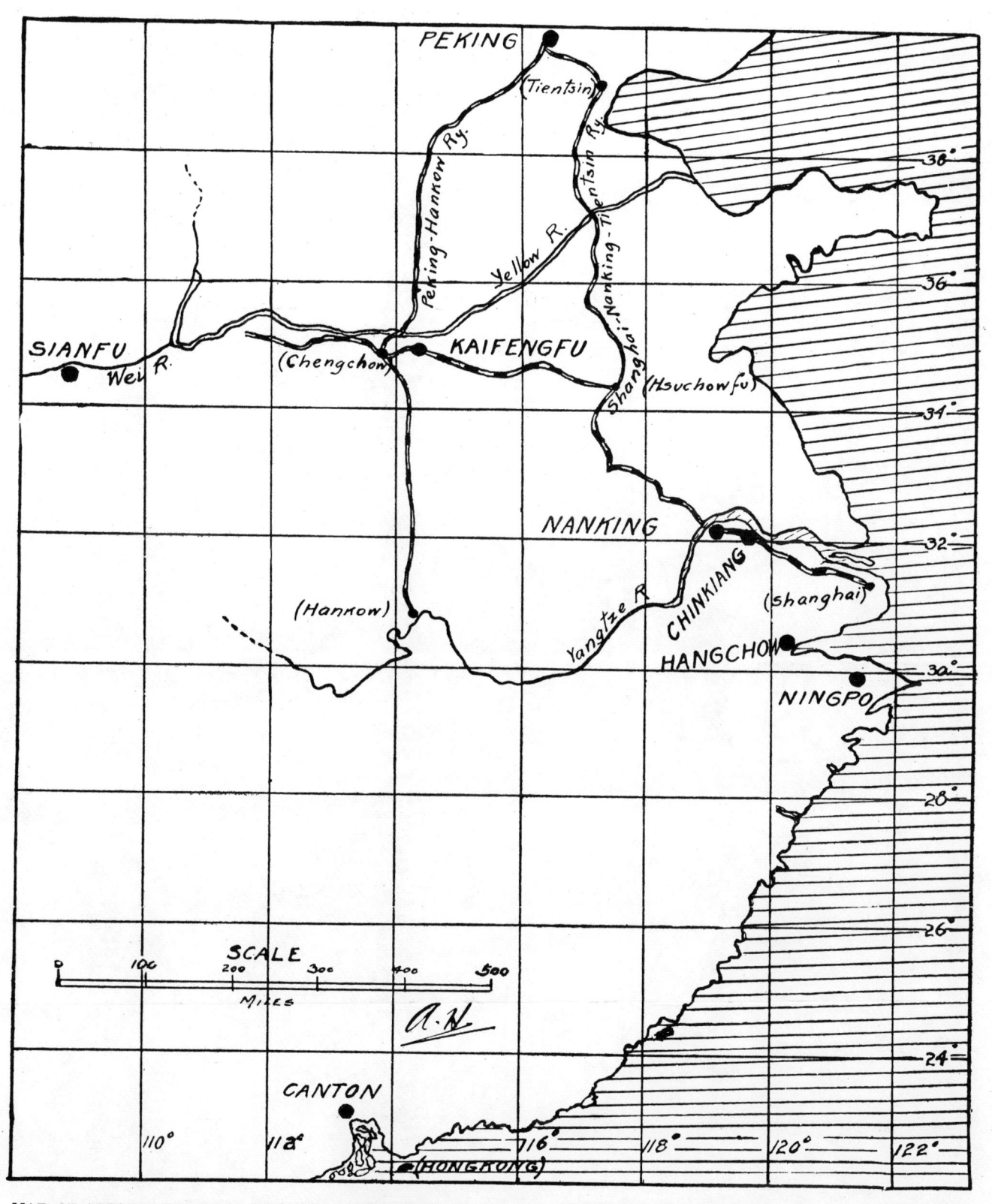

MAP OF JEWISH COLONIES IN CHINA (INDICATED BY CAPITAL LETTERS). THE TOWNS NOTED IN PARENTHESIS ARE GIVEN FOR REFERENCE PURPOSES.

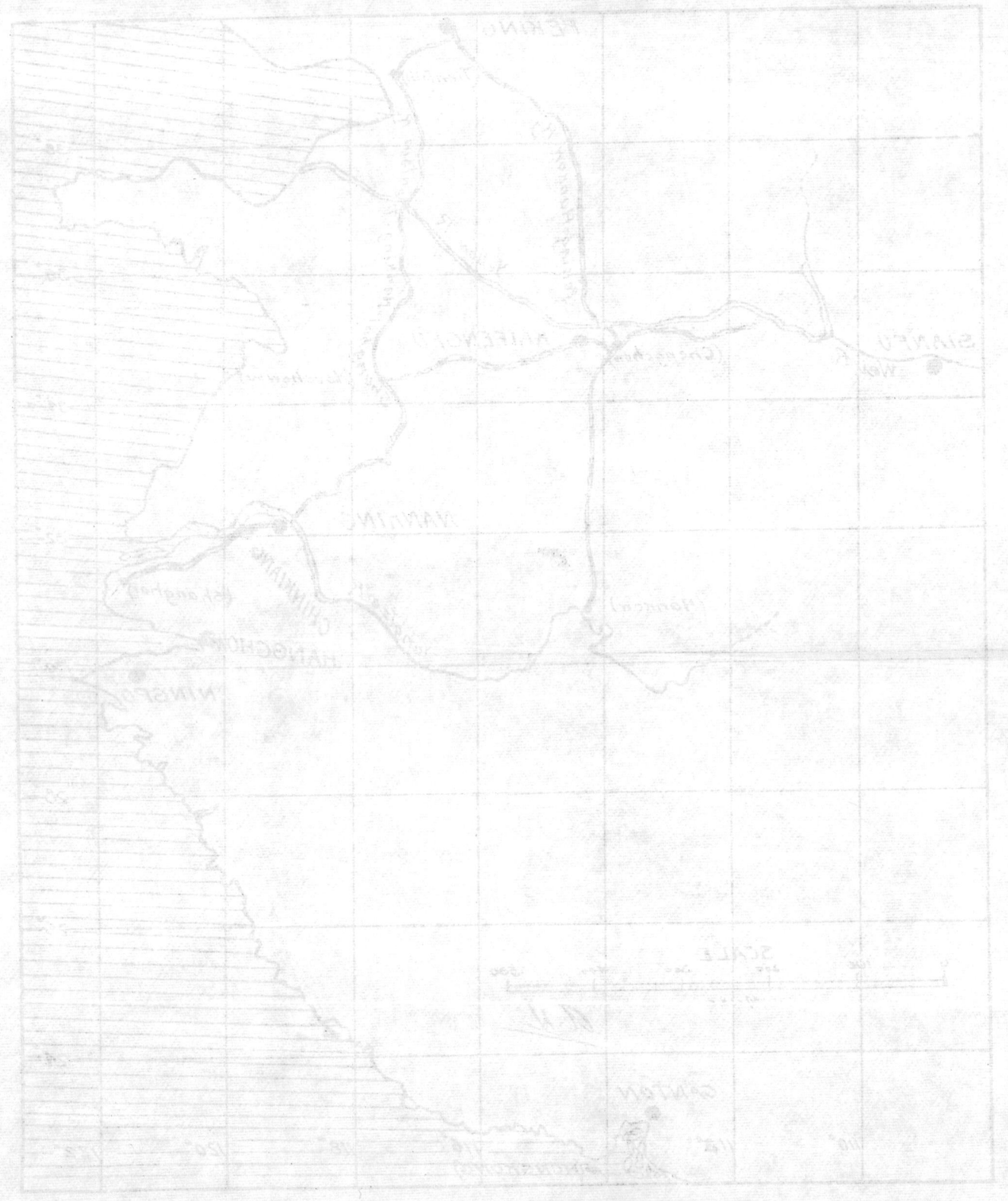

# CHINESE JEWS

*Edward I. Ezra & Arthur Sopher*

Printed by THE CHINA PRESS

## PREFACE

The widespread dispersion of the Jewish race over the face of the earth could not be better exemplified than in the presence to-day of Chinese Jews in Kaifeng-fu. No more effective proof could be desired of the virility of the race and its resistance to assimilation by other peoples than the significant fact that even in a vast country like China, the small Jewish colony in Kaifeng had for a long time withstood absorption, though it must have been at the cost of untold privations. The Jews of Kaifeng may conceivably be the remnants of those who probably branched out to this region of Asia following the Diaspora, while other groups settled elsewhere in the world. An alternative theory that may suggest itself to some is that China may really, after all, be the cradle of the human race and the repository of the world's oldest civilization. This view is supported by some singular points of similarity between the Chinese and Jewish way of life, for instance, the striking resemblance to the Jewish religious rite of "Kadeesh" (prayer for the soul of the departed), while another thing in common between the two races is the practice of keeping the head covered at all times. The Chinese long gown also is very much like the Jewish "joobba". Other points of similarity could be mentioned at random did space permit. An extension of the theme opens up an interesting and almost limitless field for speculation which can scarcely be traversed within the narrow limits of a brief preface.

When it is remembered to what an extent Jewish brains have contributed to the sum of the world's culture, when we recall how the graces of civilization in the realms of art, science and industry have been enriched by the contributions of Jews in these respective fields, one cannot but marvel at the apathy generally manifested by Jews towards the question of the rescue of the Chinese Jews. The appeal for the rebuilding of the Synagogue for the benefit of the ancient Jewish colony at Kaifengfu has so far gone more or less unheeded. This, in a sense, is a reflection on Jewry as a whole and tends to impart a semblance of justification to the oft repeated charge that Jews are solely engrossed in the pursuit of wealth and have little concern with the things of the spirit.

Dr. Martin, the veteran Protestant missionary, many years ago said that a Jewish mission was absolutely necessary and "that the rebuilding of the Synagogue is indispensable to give this colony a bond of union, and that without this nothing can save it from extinction." The claim of the Chinese Jews is well-nigh irresistible. During their prolonged existence in China, they have remained, as Dr. Martin says, like "a great rock, rent from the sides of Mount Zion by some great national catastrophe and projected into the central plain of China, which has stood there, while the centuries rolled by, sublime in its antiquity and solitude."

During the past three-quarters of a century, there have been various attempts to bring spiritual and material help to the stricken colony. About the middle of the last century, attempts in that direction were made both in England and in America. With that irony of fate, however, that frequently rules the affairs of men, misfortune has dogged the efforts of those who have interested themselves in the fate of the Chinese Jews. In England, the leader of the proposed expedition died. In America, the Civil War came and put a stop to all proceedings. If this little brochure succeeds in reviving interest in the question to the end of something tangible being accomplished, the object of the compilers will have been attained.

Even at this late hour, something can still be done to save the Chinese Jews from utter extinction. In any other country in the world, the process of absorption of Jews would have been a matter of slow progress In China, however, they faced the greatest imaginable foe—the Chinese power for assimilation of alien races, which at once makes such a thing as conquest of the Chinese impossible. Perhaps the most convincing example of this power of assimilation possessed by the Chinese race is to be found in its absorption of a considerable Jewish immigration. For a long time the Chinese Jews maintained their separate existence and the forms of their temple service. Now, and for many generations, they have been Chinese, preserving only the legend of their origin and some relics of their sacred rolls, which they are unable to understand. No other race in the world, as Dr. Charles Levermore recently reminded us in a thoughtful article, has been able to absorb this strong-fibred Semitic stock. The wonder, indeed, is not that the Chinese

Jews have virtually lost their racial identity but that they have withstood the process of assimilation so long.

The foregoing thoughts have been suggested by re-reading an informative article on the Chinese Jews which was first published in the East of Asia Magazine, is now reprinted in these pages, with an Appendix bringing the whole matter up to date. With the revival of interest in the Jewish question within recent years following the transaction in Palestine, the article is commended to those who take an intelligent interest in the affairs of unquestionably the most remarkable race in the world.

Arthur Sopher.

Shanghai, 3rd Feb. 1926.

# Chinese Jews.

A COMPREHENSIVE glance at the career of the Jewish people reveals to the student an astonishing history, full of intense picturesque traits. Since the destruction of the Hebrew Monarchy and the dispersion of the Jewish people over the face of the earth, the nation has become so widespread that Jews are to be found everywhere. This fact is familiar to all, but it is not so well known that Jews in considerable numbers have existed in China from a very remote period. In this brief essay it is my intention to give a popular account of all that I have been able to gather from numerous works on the subject. I am, of course, very much indebted to many writers both ancient and modern, and I have used their information freely.

The earliest descriptions we are able to obtain of Jews in China are from meagre incidental comments, but in the absence of any fuller details these scanty items must prove acceptable to us. From inscriptions on one of the stone tablets found in the Synagogue at Kaifengfu, capital of Honan, we are told that Jews first entered China during the Han Dynasty, from B.C. 200 to A.D. 226, and in the letters of the Jesuits we are informed that "they came during the reign of Mingti (A.D. 58 to 75) from Siyih," ie., "the Western regions." The Jesuit fathers concluded that this Western country is Persia and that they must have come by Khorasan and Samarcand. This view I believe is correct, for the ritual we find established amongst the Chinese Jews clearly comes by way of Persia. There are many Persian words in their language and literature, and their hymns as well as other poetry compare favourably with those found in old Persian MS. prayer-books. Many writers have expressed their opinion that these Jews are descended from the ten lost tribes. This view cannot be accepted, as there is no tangible evidence warranting it; we only know they have probably come by way of Persia. A work of the Sung Dynasty by Sung Tsze-aou, entitled the "Tung King Ke," reported that in the city of Kaifengtu there was a heaven-spirit monastery, and this being about the third or fourth century A.D. is the earlist record of the sect in Chinese works.

In another work published by Wei Shuh we find reference to a "foreign heaven chapel" in the city of Changngan in Shensi, which was erected in the year A.D. 621 The "Chang Ngan Che," by Min Kew of the Sung Dynasty, commenting on this chapel, says there was an officer called "Sapaou" who managed the services of this place of worship. The word Sapaou is not a Chinese word and reminds one of the Hebrew saupher or sopher, a scribe, and in later times we have much evidence of the importance of these officials among the Israelites in China.

In 878, Abou Zeyd Al Hassan, an Arabian writer, enumerates the Jews as one of the sects who perished in a general massacre which occurred at Khanfu. In 956 and 958, we find the district officials of Kaifengfu conferring marks of honour on the Jews residing there, and about the year 1163 the erection of a Synagogue was commenced in that town. In 1279 one of the inscriptions in the Synagogue informs us that the ancient place of worship was rebuilt on a larger and superior scale. From some casual observations in Marco

Polo's Travels we learn that the Israelites were sufficiently numerous about this time to maintain political influence in China and Tartary. In the Chinese records the Jews are spoken of in 1329 and again in 1354 as having been invited to Pekin to join the Imperial army, which shows that they must have been numerous enough to make their help in men and means necessary to the government. They are styled Shuhwuh or Jehudi, but nothing is mentioned as to their place of residence.

About the year 1346, the Arabian envoy, Ibn Batuta, refers to the existence of Jews in China and says "their great men are exceedingly wealthy." In 1445, Kaifengfu was a great city containing, some say, over a million inhabitants, and it appears that this city from its commercial importance soon became the headquarters of the Chinese Jews. In 1461, the overflowing of the Yellow River almost destroyed the whole Synagogue; by official consent it was considerably enlarged towards the end of the fifteenth century, and a record of the event was preserved on a stone erected in 1489. Another stone tablet was erected in 1512, giving a summary of the religious views of the sect at that period. We find a reference to the Jews about this time in the writings of Parera, an Italian, who was for many year a prisoner in the hands of the Chinese.

From numerous records there is sufficient ground for believing that in the fifteenth century there were numerous communities of Jews in China, as many references are found pointing to establishments in Ningpo, Hangchow, and Pekin.

The earliest reliable and authoritative accounts of the Jews in China we owe to the Jesuits who, at the close of the sixteenth century, had just obtained a residence in Pekin. Before the detailed observations of the Jesuits reached Europe, the European Jews were completely ignorant of the existence of a colony of their co-religionists in China, and the Chinese Jews were equally unaware of their foreign brethren. It was in the days of Queen Elizabeth that the Church of Rome sent out to China a band of missionaries who were not only well received at Pekin but raised to high posts in the Empire. Father Ricci, one of the first of these missionaries, in his report to the Vatican gives us an extremely interesting account of how he discovered the existence of Jews in China. Early in the seventeenth century, one summer's day in Pekin, a visitor, prompted by rumours of the arrival of certain foreigners who worshipped a single God and yet were not Mohammedans, called on Father Ricci. The missionary, noticing the difference of features from the ordinary Chinese, led him to the oratory and knelt on his kness before a picture of the Virgin with the infant Jesus, and St. John the Baptist. Near by was another picture representing four of the apostles. The visitor knelt also, remarking, "We in China do reverence our ancestors. This is Rebecca with her sons Jacob and Esau; but as to the other picture, why make obeisance to only four sons of Jacob; were there not twelve?" Returning to the former apartment mutual explanations followed and an unforeseen solution ensued. The stranger was a Hebrew, Ngai by name, who had come to Pekin from Kaifengfu to procure literary honours. He stated that in his city there some twelve families of Israelites with a fair synagogue in which they preserved a Roll of the Law over four hundred years old, and in Hangchow, the capital of Chekiang, there were many more families also with a synagogue. Scattered over the length and breadth of China there were others of his sect, but these were gradually being lost from having no meeting place. When shown a Bible in Hebrew he confessed his inability to read it, though he recognized the characters.

THE THRONE OF MOSES.

He said that his preference for Gentile literature subjected him to many reproaches from the Chief of the Synagogue. Father Ricci was able to test the truth of these statements and despatched some Chinese Christian messengers to Kaifengfu for purposes of investigation, and soon received visits from other native Jews.

The first European we hear of visiting the colony was Julius Aleni, in 1613, and he confirmed all that was previously ascertained.

Sammedo, writing in 1642, reported Jews living in four Chinese towns and that they were highly esteemed by their fellow citizens. In 1642 the Synagogue at Kaifengfu was again devastated by the Yellow River and a great number of valuable manuscript books were lost. During the eighteenth century several Europeans were admitted to see the synagogue, but the best account we possess is from the pen of Gozani. In a letter dated Kaifengfu, November, 1704, we are given full details of Jewish customs and a description of the communal buildings.

From Gozani's statement it appears that the sect was known as the "Taoukin Kiao"; i.e., "the sect that plucks out the sinews." This refers to a command in Gen. xxxii. 32. and is universally adopted by orthodox Jews everywhere. On his arrival he made them protestations of friendship to which they readily responded and called on him at his inn. He returned their visit at the "Lepai

Tze," as they called their Synagogue, where he was received with great ceremony, and was shown numerous inscriptions in Hebrew and Chinese which they allowed him to copy. They showed him their religious books and took him all over the sacred edifice, even to places where the Rabbi only had right of access. From Gozani's communication it would appear that a charitable spirit and friendly bearing distinguished the whole community.

The curiosity of Europeans being stirred up by this and other descriptions, some time after, Domenge sketched a plan of the communal buildings, while Gaubil procured translations and copies of many inscriptions on the walls and other monumental stones. From accounts and information given by the Jesuits, to whom we are indebted for nearly all our present knowledge of the Chinese Jews, we are able to give a full description of the Synagogue and other buildings at Kaifengfu as they appeared in the latter part of the eighteenth century. The sacred edifice, named Tsing Chin Tze, or "Pure and True Temple," filled up a space of some four hundred feet in length by about one hundred and fifty feet in breadth, comprising a large establishment consisting of four separate courts, various buildings for residence, worship, and work. The first court had in its centre a triumphal arch decorated with a golden inscription dedicating the whole structure to the Creator Preserver of all things.

The second court is entered from the first by a large gate with two side doors. Its walls are flanked on the north and south by dwellings for the keepers of the sacred place. In the centre of the third court stood an arch like that of the first court.

Marble tablets with inscriptions in Chinese (Paiwan) ornamented the walls. A section of this court is flanked by memorial chapels; that in the south in memory of a Jewish Mandarin named Chao, and on the north in remembrance of him who constructed the present building. There are also several reception-rooms for guests. The fourth court is parted in two by a row of trees. Half way along this line stood a huge brazen vase for incense, at each side of which were two marble lions on pedestals and two brazen vases containing flowers.

Contiguous to the northern wall was a recess in which the nerves and sinews were extracted from animals slaughtered for food. The second division of the court was an empty space with a hall of ancestors (Tsutang) at each of its sides, north and south. Here were venerated at the vernal and autumnal equinoxes, after the Chinese style, the heroes of Biblical history, each having his name without any picture recorded on a tablet. The chief furniture were large censers in honour of Abraham and smaller ones for Isaac, Jacob, the twelve sons of Jacob, also Moses, Aaron, Joshua, and Ezra. In the open space just mentioned, between the two halls of ancestors, it was customary to erect the booth of boughs at the annual Feast of Tabernacles.

The Lepai Tze, or Synagogue, measured about sixty by forty feet, having a portico with a double row of four columns before it. In the centre of the room between the rows of pillars stood the Throne of Moses, a magnificent and elevated chair with an embroidered cushion, upon which they placed the Book of the Law when it was read. In front of this pulpit was a tablet (Wansuipai) with the Emperor's name in golden characters.

Over this a dome was suspended surmounted by an inscription in Hebrew. On a large table by the door was placed six candelabra in one line, with a great vase for incense, and a tablet recording the acts of kindness of the sovereigns of the Ming Dynasty who had given directions for the burning of the incense. Situated at the western extremity of the chamber was the Tien Tang—house of heaven—or Bethel, as the Jesuits called it, square in shape but rounded within. Into this none but the Rabbi may enter during the time of prayer. Here on separate tables were the twelve Rolls of the Law corresponding to the twelve Tribes of Israel, in addition to one in the centre in honour of Moses; each enclosed in separate silken curtains. The scroll in the centre was highly venerated, and it is affirmed that all the other scrolls were merely copies of the venerated one. On the western wall two tablets were prominent, and on them were inscribed the Ten Commandments. By the side of these were tables containing manuscript books, and a table bearing a vase and two candelabra.

Among their religious customs we observe worshippers took off their shoes on entering the house of prayer, and wore a blue headdress while there, in opposition to the Mohammedans, who wore white. When reading the Law the minister covered his face with a transparent evil of gauze in imitation of Moses, who brought the Law to the Israelites with his face covered. They also wore a red silk scarf depending from the right shoulder and tied under the left arm. By the side of the reader stood a monitor to rectify his reading if necessary, who was in like manner attended by another monitor. The prayers were chanted, but with no musical instruments. The congregation wore no garment of fringes or "sisith" during the service, as is always done by the Jews in other parts of world. They adhered to the law of circumcision and kept the various Festivals of the Tabernacles, Passover, and especially the Day of Atonement; for it is said that on certain days of the year they fasted and wept together in the Synagogue. They were never allowed to intermarry with the heathen and made no converts. They never pronounced the sacred name of God, but said Adonai instead. They held to the unity of God, but otherwise had no articles of belief, at the same time giving credence to vague theories of heaven, hell, purgatory, the resurrection of the dead, the day of judgment, and the influences of angels, evil spirits, devils, and other monsters of the imagination. In prayer they turned westwards towards Jerusalem; the Sabbath they observed with great severity, food being prepared the day before. Their customs and usages correspond favourably with those in vogue among the Jews of the present day, even their calendar being identical.

As already mentioned, the Synagogue at Kaifengfu possessed thirteen Rolls of the Law kept within coverings of silk. In addition to this were a number of square books (not Rolls) which were classified as follows:—

1.—Ta King, in fifty-three books, each containing one section of the Law for Sabbath days.

2.—Tsin Sou, or supplementary books; called also Hafootala (Haphtara). These are portions of Joshua, Judges, Samuel, Kings, and the Prophets.

3.—Historical books, viz:—Esther, Ezra, Nehemiah, Chronicles, and the two Books of Maccabees.

4.—Keang Chang, or the Expositors. These are much defaced, and the short leisure of the Jesuits prevented a close examination of this section.

5.—Le Pai, the ritual or ceremonial books, about fifty in number. These books were all jealously guarded, and Gozani in his first letter said, "All these books are preserved with greater care than gold or silver."

They were generally kept in repositories at the Synagogue and never allowed to be taken home. One Ngai Wen promised for a sum of money to procure Father Domenge a volume of Tsin, Sou, but he was detected, and made to retire with shame with the proverb, "He who sells his Scripture sells his God." It is stated that when a rich man bestows a copy of the Law on the Synagogue, the worth of the present is rated so high as to set aside all need of attending Divine service during the rest of his life.

The people showed very little desire to compare their Scriptures with those presented by the Jesuits. In one instance only, Gaubil relates, comparing with a Rabbi the names and ages of the patriarchs in the genealogies from

Adam to Noah, and in these they found a complete agreement.

In reading and writing Hebrew, the Jews were generally ignorant, though by persevering repetition they were able to read the Old Testament with facility of expression, but only by means of Chinese pronunciation. They appeared anxious to hear their missionary visitors read with European pronunciation. The Sacred Rolls had no vowel points; the minor books already enumerated were written in larger characters containing vowel points, stops, and accents. The small or larger letters occasionally met with in the Hebrew text they preserved with punctilious exactness. The Song of Moses in Deut. xxxii is written in double columns and all the books have their titles on the first page written within a square of blue, green, or white lines.

The chief facts and traditions concerning the remote history of the Israelites in China are chiefly deduced from four important inscriptions in Chinese upon the marble tablets of the Synagogue. Père Tobar has published an extremely valuable work on these inscriptions, entitled "Inscriptions Juives de Kaifengfu," and this work contains a reproduction and translation into French of the inscriptions on the stone tablets dated 1489, 1512, and 1663. I here give abstracts from Père Tobar's book of these dated stone steles which, though rather lengthy for this paper, yet are essential to a right understanding of the Orphan Colony.

I. ABSTRACT OF INSCRIPTION ON STONE STELE OF 1489.

Abraham was the nineteenth in descent from Adam.

The patriarchs handed down the tradition forbidding the making and worshipping of images and spirits, and the holding of superstitions. Abraham pondered over problems of nature and arrived at the belief in the true God and became the founder of the religion we believe in to this day. This happened in the 146th year of the Tcheou Dynasty.

His belief was handed down from father to son till Moses, who, it is found, was alive in the 613th year of the Tcheou Dynasty. He was endowed with wisdom and virtue. He abode forty days on the summit of Mount Sinai, refraining from meat and drink, and communing with God. The fifty-three portions of the Law had their origin with him. From him the law and traditions were handed down unto Ezra, who was likewise a patriarch.

Man in his daily pursuits must ever have God before him. We pray three times a day; morning, noon, and evening.

Four days every month are devoted to purification and to stimulating to charitable acts. Every seventh day is devoted to rest, and a fresh period of good deeds then commences. In the fourth season of the year the Jew places himself under severe restraint for seven days. One entire day he abstains altogether from food, devoting it to prayer and repentance. Our religion came originally from Tienchuh.

[**Note.**—The designation Tienchuh is generally translated "India," but Syria appears formerly to have been included under the same term, and Dr. Wylie says there is no doubt that Syria is intended here.]

Seventy families, viz., Li, Yen, Kao, Tchao, and others, came to the Court of Song bringing, as tribute, cloth of cotton from Western lands. The Emperor said, "You have come to China. Keep and follow the customs of your forefathers and settle at Pienlang" (Kaifengfu). In the first year of Long Hing of the Sung Dynasty (1163), when Liwei (Levi) was the Ouseta (Rabbi), Yentula erected the Synagogue. Under the Yuen Dynasty (1279) the temple structure was rebuilt.

The Emperor Tai Tsou, who founded the Ming Dynasty, granted in 1390, to all who submitted to his authority, land on which they could dwell peacefully and profess their religion without molestation.

In the nineteenth year of Yong Lo (1421), Yen Tcheng, a physician, received from the Emperor a present of incense and permission to repair the Synagogue.

In 1461 there was an overflow of the Yellow River and the foundations alone of the structure were left standing.

Later on, the cells of the Synagogue were put up and three copies of the Holy Law were placed there. Various dignitaries presented articles and other furniture for Israel's temple called Itzelonietien.

All this has been recorded, to be handed down to the latest generations by me, Kin Tchong, literary graduate in the second year of Hong Tche (1489).

II   INSCRIPTION ON STONE STELE OF 1512.

Erected by Tsou Tang, a mandarin, on the occasion when a copy of the Law was presented by Kin Pou of Weiyang. The following passage is of interest:—"After the Creation the Doctrine was transmitted by Adam to Noah; thence unto Abraham, Isaac and Jacob, and afterwards through the twelve patriarchs to Moses, Aaron, and Joshua. Ezra promulgated the Law, and through him the letters of the Yuethe, (Yehudi) Jewish nation, were made plain."

III.   INSCRIPTION ON STONE STELE OF 1668.

In a long preamble an attempt is made to show that there is nothing in the Sacred Law of the Jews which is not in conformity with the six canonical books of the Chinese. Then follow notices of the Jewish settlement. A graphic account is given of the events which followed the fall of the Ming Dynasty in 1642.

We will be able to comprehend the substantial information given us by the Jesuits when we realize that, about the end of the eighteenth century, the decline of the Jewish colony was so rapid that it became only a question of time for the whole community to collapse, which break-down occurred during the first quarter of the nineteenth century. From this time no authentic information could be got from them, except details from hearsay. In 1777 and 1779, Olave Tychsen, the learned Orientalist, sent Hebrew letters to Kaifengfu, but no information has ever been received that they reached their destination. In 1815 some Jews in London sent a letter through Dr. Morrison, and there is good reason to believe that it reached them, but no reply was received. The account of Gozani and other missionaries from the Church of Rome remained as the latest information until Dr. Smith, Bishop of Hongkong, despatched a deputation of two trustworthy Chinese to obtain all possible details regarding the colony.

The messengers started from Shanghai on November 15th, 1850, and journeyed by way of the Grand Canal and Yellow River. After a tedious journey of 25 days they arrived at their destination on December 9th, and immediately began their search for the ancient people. They easily discovered the place and found the whole structure in ruins.

Within the precinct of the temple were a number of small apartments, all inhabited by Israelites, and on asking them "How many people live here? and is the teacher (Rabbi) still alive?" they said, "We, who belong to this religion, are the only people who live here, and our teacher is now no more; our temple is all ruined and we are nearly starved." On being questioned, "Are there any who can read the Hebrew character?" they said, "Formerly there were some who could, but now all have been scattered abroad and there is not one who can read it." Next day the messengers from Shanghai were allowed, on account of the Hebrew letter of introduction they had with them, to examine the sacred buildings. They were told that several strangers had before tried to gain admittance but were refused permission to enter. Directly behind the front door stood a bench, about six feet from which was a long stand for candles; immediately in connection with this was a table, in the centre of which was placed an earthenware incense-vessel having a wooden candlestick at each end. In the centre of the building rested a structure resembling a pulpit; then the Wan-suipai, or Emperor's Tablet, placed on a large

Table in a shrine adorned with the usual formula:—"May the Manchu Dynasty retain the Imperial sway through myriads and myriads and ten thousand myriads of years!" Above the Emperor's tablet was the following inscription in Hebrew:—

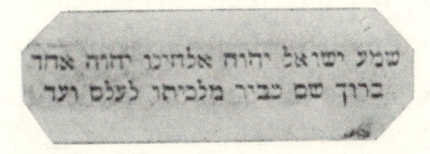

שמע ישראל יהוה אלהינו יהוה אחד
ברוך שם כבוד מלכותו לעלם ועד

> Hear O Israel! the Lord is our God,
> The Lord is One!
>
> Blessed be the name of the glory of His Kingdom for ever and ever.

A little way off was a cell in which were deposited the Sacred Writings, and to the right and left of the holy cell were other cells each bearing the following inscription in Hebrew:—

קמון    שמש
שמע ישראל יהוה
אלהינו יהוה אחד
ברוך שם כבוד
מלכותו לעלם ועד

SHEMESH.    KAMON.

(**Note.**—Shemesh and Kamon are the names of two angels.)

Hear O Israel! the Lord

Is our God! The Lord is One!
Blessed be the name of the glory
Of His Kingdom for ever and ever!

While engaged in copying the above a man named Kiao came and drove the Shanghai deputation unceremoniously out of the temple, saying in a loud voice, "These men are sent from the English missionaries to examine our establishment and you must not let them come here any more." The result of all these inquiries confirmed in every respect all previous accounts; but the community was in a deplorable state. Although the messengers were suddenly interrupted in their researches in the Synagogue, and their departure from the city was hastened by fear, they were able to copy numerous inscriptions in Chinese and Hebrew. The following are a few examples of tablets hung from pillars as is usual in Chinese temples:—

路正德道遠不親師君地天得識
流源賢聖是便信智禮義仁在修

If you acknowledge heaven, earth, prince, parent, and teacher, you will not be far from the correct road to reason and virtue.

If you cultivate the duties of benevolence, righteousness, propriety, wisdom, and truth, you have just hit upon the first principles of sages and philosophers.

本之人生地天生生求靈鐘笠西來以化嬋媧女自
全人道學釋學儒學得教衍華中後而宗開羅阿由

From the time of Nuwa (Eve), when the beauteous creation sprang into being, up to the present time, Western Syria has had men of natural talent who have inquired into the Great Original that produced heaven, earth, and man.

From the time of Alo (Abraham), when our religion was first established, and ever afterwards, China has diffused instruction and obtained the knowledge of the whole system propagated by Confucius, Buddha, and Lautze.

祖念而因天敬天承獨祖
生存以所殺戒殺止能生

Our first ancestor received his religion from God, and honoured God (Heaven) alone, which feeling we carry out to the venerating of our forefathers.

The Living One prohibited killing and forbade murder, to show his regard for human life.

Early next year the two Chinese messengers again visited Kaifengfu to procure additional MSS., and also to bring down any Jews who might be induced to visit Shanghai. They returned on the 20th July, 1851, bringing numerous Rolls of the Law. Some difficulty was experienced when they invited two Israelites to accompany them down, but after great deliberation their proposal was agreed to. It took a fortnight to persuade the Jews at Kaifengfu to part with some of the sacred Rolls. At length a meeting of the elders was held in the Synagogue and a number of beautiful Rolls in good preservation handed over in the presence of all. The messengers, having at last received the much-coveted treasure, wisely determined on an immediate departure and left next morning with two Chinese Jews. Each of the Rolls contained a complete copy of the Books of Moses. They were beautifully written on white sheepskin, cut and sewed together, about twenty and thirty yards long and rolled on sticks. In addition to the large Rolls, they received a great number of smaller manuscripts and these were not written on parchment but on thick yellowish paper. Among them were several containing the services for the Day of Atonement and others entitled the "Hundred Blessings" for the same day. Another had, at the end of it, the names of the Jewish months and days of the week. Considering everything there is no doubt that the Jews of Kaifengfu have been loyal guardians of the Law.

The two Jews who came to Shanghai were named Chau Wan-kwei and Chau Kin-ching; besides these Chinese names they had no Hebrew ones. The elder was about forty-five, the younger about thirty. They were both circumcised, and stated that circumcision was still practised in Kaifengfu. They called the rite "mila," which is the same Hebrew name given to it by Jews in other parts of the world. On being shown a map of Jerusalem and the Holy Temple, they mentioned that they had seen a drawing similar to this in their Synagogue, which their forefathers said belonged to the country from which they came. They studied Hebrew with the intention of returning to teach others; but nothing came of it, and I have not been able to trace what happened to these two men; probably they turned back after some time to their native city.

A transcript from one of the minor Rolls brought by Bishop Smith's messengers is in

THE TEN COMMANDMENTS, AS DESCRIBED ON THE
CODE OF LAWS, WHICH HAS BEEN BROUGHT
FROM KAIFENGFU TO SHANGHAI.

my library, and at the end of the one of the sections is the following suffix:—

HOLINESS TO JEHOVAH!

The Rabbi Akiba, the son of Aaron, the son of Ezra, collected it;

Shadior, the son of Bethuel, the son of Moses, read it;

Mordecai, the son of Moses, witnessed it;

And he believed in Jehovah; who counted it for righteousness.

The deplorable condition in which the Bishop's mission found the Jews indicated a rapid extinction of the sect. The colony had suffered much during the great inundation of the Yellow River—China's Sorrow, as it has aptly been called—in the year 1849, and the surviving two hundred individuals were found in abject ignorance, destitution and misery. So low had they fallen that many of their buildings had been sold for food to support their lives. Says Bishop Smith: "Sunk in the lowest poverty and destitution, their religion scarcely more than a name and yet sufficient to separate them from the multitude around, exposed to trial, reproach, and the pain of long deferred hope, they remained the unconscious depositories of the oracles of God surviving as the solitary witnesses of departed glory."

A Jewish Society was formed in 1852 in the United States for Jewish missions to neglected colonies. Funds were collected

CH'AU WAN-KUEI AND CH'AU KIN-CHING.

and a Committee formed, but the Civil War frustrated the undertaking. The Jewish traveller, "Benjamin II," visited England in 1864 and expressed his readiness to visit the settlement. A Society was formed with Mr. Rothschild, Mr. S. D. Sassoon, and others on the Committee, but owing to the death of Benjamin II the project was abandoned. Then the late Dr. Adler, Chief Rabbi of London (father of the present Chief Rabbi), addressed a letter to Messrs. David Sassoon, Sons & Co., Shanghai, suggesting that two youths from the settlement of Kaifengfu be brought down and educated so as to enable them to return and take up the position of Jewish ministers. Two young men were indeed chosen, but soon became homesick and returned.

In February, 1866, Dr. Martin visited the colony and learned that during the interval of fifteen years, since Dr. Smith's mission, the colony had become still more impoverished. Dr. Martin was the first Protestant who visited the settlement, and up to the date of his journey the colony had not been visited for more than two centuries by any European. On arriving at the city he was assured by some Mohammedan friends that the Synagogue had become a desolation and the worshippers impoverished and scattered abroad. "Then," said the Doctor, "I will go and see the spot on which it stood," and directing his bearers to the place he came to an open square in the centre of which stood a solitary stone. On one side was an inscription commemorating the erection of the Synagogue, on the other a record of its rebuilding. "Are there among you any of the family of Israel?" "I am one," responded a young man whose face, Dr. Martin says, corroborated his assertion. There on the melancholy spot where the very foundations of the Synagogue had been torn from the ground, they confessed with shame to their visitor, that their holy and beautiful house had been demolished by their own hands from the pressure of necessity. They estimated their number at from three to four hundred poverty-stricken souls and, now that the Synagogue had disappeared, likely to become scattered and, as a community, wiped out. One had lately become a priest of Buddha, taking for his title "Pentao" signifying "one who is rooted in the knowledge of truth." The large tablet that once ornamented the entrance of the holy edifice, consisting of the name "Israel" (Itzelonetien) in gilded characters, had been placed in a mosque, and some of their brethren had turned Mohammedans. They were called by the inhabitants "sinew-pickers," a name given them in derision. Though they still preserved several copies of the Law there was no one competent to read them, and not long before it was seriously proposed to exhibit their parchments in the market place, in the hope that they might attract the attention of some travelling Jew who might be able to restore to them the language of their forefathers. One

THE LAST COMMEMORATIVE STONE.

of them confessed his wife was a heathen; another said that although they remembered the Feast of Tabernacles, the Passover, and a few ceremonies, these were now so neglected that scarcely any one carried them out or even remembered how to observe them. There is no doubt that the Taiping Rebellion had sadly told on the town of Kaifengfu, and the Jews, owing to the nature of their employments, had, perhaps, undergone the greatest misery. Many had moved away permanently from the town and had thus been lost to the community. Three years later (1869), Dr. Martin addressed a latter to the editor of the "Jewish Times", of New York, embodying his observations and proposing the formation of a Jewish mission. The appeal excited some discussion among the Jews, but, unfortunately, produced no further result than the sending to the Doctor of sundry letters in Hebrew with a request to forward them to a people who had forgotten the language of their ancestors.

Whilst residing at Peking, Herr J. L. Libermann was informed that there were still some five hundred Chinese Jews left. This induced him to pay them a visit, which he did in July, 1857, being the first, and I believe the only, Jew from the outside world that visited this neglected colony. He wrote a long letter of what he saw to his father in Beilitz. He explored the fields of ruins in all directions; they appear to have covered an area of 300 feet in length and 150 feet in breadth. He was taken round the ruined temple and then conducted to the cellar of a house. There his guide removed, from a vault underneath, three granite slabs covering as many chests of ironlike wood, heavier and certainly more durable than the metal. Incased in pieces of thick soft silk he saw numerous papyri and parchment rolls, of which the oldest he thought to be within

THE SITE IN KAIFENGFU WHERE ONCE THE SYNAGOGUE STOOD.

twenty or twenty-three centuries old, but which, probably, could not have been more than four or five hundred years old at the very highest computation. Before leaving he made a hasty survey of the Jewish quarter and found the settlement numbering from 400 to 500 individuals, in the midst of poverty and wretchedness. He was told that some Jews still kept the Sabbath and, in a room set aside for weekly prayer meetings, he found the Ten Commandments engraved on a tablet, and the following Confession of Faith on a stone slab:—

We believe that Adam was the first man. Abraham was the founder of our religion. After him came Moses, who gave us laws and the Holy Scriptures. Those trying to picture the Lord in stone, or in other ways, are wasting their time.

Those who honour the Holy Scriptures and obey them will learn the origin of things, for the Scriptures tell whence man's life has spring.

Every one professing the Hebrew faith must try to do good and avoid doing evil, if he would be worthy to bear the name of a Jew.

In August, 1891, Mr. Dennis J. Mills visited the spot, and the first person of whom he inquired told him that about 200 families were scattered over the city. He visited the site of the tabernacle and found it partly a rubbish heap and partly a pool of water. A stone tablet in the centre served to preserve the site as the property of the Jewish community. He

LI KING SHENG AND HIS SON LI TSUNG-MAI.

could hardly help weeping at seeing the desolation of the spot.

On the 28th December, 1899, Dr. Timothy Richard wrote a letter to an old Jewish resident of Shanghai pointing out to him that some Hebrew manuscripts had been purchased by the Jesuits at Kaifengfu and brought down to Shanghai. This prompted a party of Jewish residents, including the writer, to visit the Sicawei Observantory for the purpose of inspecting the manuscript. The result was the formation of a Society for the rescue of these Chinese Jews. Meetings were held for the purpose of collecting reliable information and some Protestant Missionaries very kindly undertook to do their best to help the Committee. Through their instrumentality a letter in Hebrew and Chinese, signed by forty-six members of the Jewish Community in Shanghai, was sent some time in August, 1900. The first copy of the letter, dated March 13th, was destroyed by a party of Boxers when looting one of the Protestant missions. The second copy reached its destination in due course, and on the 24th October, 1900, a reply was received to the effect that the war with the foreigners, and the disquieting rumours, from the North, kept a

THE DEPUTATION OF EIGHT JEWS FROM KAIFENGFU IN 1902.

few from coming down. An answer was immediately despatched asking one or two to make an effort to come down at once. The result of this message was the arrival, on the 6th April, 1901, of our messenger, together with a Chinese Jew named Li King-sheng and his son Li Tsung-mai, a youth of some twelve years of age. Residing here for about three weeks they left with another letter from the Rescue Society asking for a representative deputation to visit their foreign co-religionists. Towards the end of January this year, a letter was received from the Chinese Jew, Li King-sheng, informing the Jewish Community that he intended to visit them next spring with some of his friends, and a month later a telegram was received, dated 22nd February, saying "Eight Jews left yesterday." They arrived in Shanghai on the 10th March, this year (1902), and were very well received.

With the kind help of a friend, a meeting with these eight Chinese Jews was held at my residence on Wednesday evening, March 26th, when I subjected them to a thorough cross-examination lasting over two hours. The information I was able to elicit I embodied in a report to the Rescue Society. From the answers to a number of questions put by me it appears that they regard themselves as quite separate from the Chinese.-Questioned as to whether any of them knew anything of their religion, they said that for a long period before

THE BOY ISRAEL AND HIS BROTHER.

the Taiping rebellion they were gradually declining and their faith was rapidly being forgotten. At present they do not observe any of the ordinances of the Jewish religion, nor do they observe the idolatrous practices of the heathen.

Some years before the Taiping rebllion, in the 21st year of the Emperor Tao Kwang, there was a tremendous flood, which spread such awful devastation that many perished. This flood, coupled with the rebellion, broke them up so completely that the new generation was brought up in utter ignorance of everything connected with their religion and history. From the most ancient times they were divided into seven clans, viz., Kou, Shoa, Ia, Li, Shu, Kin, and Chong; every Chinese Jew living today is a member of one of these clans, and outside these families there are no other people of their race. Those who have come to Shanghai are representatives of four of these clans and the oldest man amongst them possesses a family record running through a period of over two hundred years. With regard to the number of Jews still remaining, they stated that quite a number had gone away from Kaifengfu and thus been lost, but those that they knew of, who are members of these seven clans, do not number more than one hundred and forty adults. They are at present in such a deplorable condition that they have no leader, no

Synagogue, and no school in which to educate their children. Most of them have been very much ashamed at the ruined condition prevailing, but what could they do?

With regard to their Synagogue, they have been told by their fathers that once upon a time they had a place of worship which was the heart of their community, but for a considerable period the buildings have been completely destroyed. The ground on which the Synagogue was erected used to be in the name of one of their people, but at the time of the rebellion the title deeds were lost. About four years ago they applied to the local authorities for new deeds; after some difficulty their application was granted and they now hold title deeds for the site. According to their statement the ground measures 200 mow, but this is impossible and I am afraid I misunderstood them. The site is now a water hole, with a stone standing in the centre, a solitary witness to their departed glory. There are a few traditional commands they still remember and are trying to observe. They are under no circumstances allowed to consider Mohammedans as the same race, nor to use heathen musical instruments in marriage. They are to take out the sinews before preparing meat for food, and are forbidden to eat pork. One man stated that he remembered his father telling him that in olden days when they entered the Synagogue they always took off their shoes and wore caps. The treatment they receive from the Chinese Government is no better and no worse than the rest of the inhabitants. They affirmed with frankness that in coming to Shanghai they are not prompted by the hope of personal gain; they are quite satisfied with their lot from a material standpoint; their chief desire is to be instructed in the religion of their forefathers. Their leader closed the interview by expressing a hope that the Synagogue in Kaifengfu may soon be rebuilt and the remnants of the ancient settlement once more rejuvenated. "And this," he continued "can only be done with the assistance of our foreign brethren We are desirous of being instructed—teach us, and raise us from the dust!" From all appearance these men show great sincerity and their honesty was further proved when one of their number proposed and then allowed his eldest son, aged fifteen years, to be circumcised, which ceremony was successfully performed on the 27th May last. The lad was named Israel and he is now receiving instruction.

Of the eight Jews who visited us four have returned, provided with some copies of the Old Testament in Chinese. Thus the matter stands at present.

We have seen that, after a prolonged struggle, the ancient colony at Kaifengfu was at its last gasp, and at this eleventh hour not a moment should be lost in saving these pitiful remnants. It is one of the most astonishing facts of history that a small settlement of Jews have been able to survive the vicissitudes of some two thousand years in the heart of a country of pagans.

The Jewish community in Shanghai, and their friends in England and on the Continent, have taken this matter in their hands; it is to be hoped that some tangible result will follow.

Dr. Martin, the veteran Protestant Missionary, says a Jewish Mission is absolutely necessary and "that the rebuilding of the Synagogue is indispensable to give this Colony a bond of union, and that without this nothing can save it from extinction." Dr. Martin is quite right. It is highly essential that arrangements be made without delay for the rebuilding of the Synagogue, the site of which, as we have seen, is still in the Colony's name. During their prolonged existence in China they have indeed remained, as Dr. Martin says, like "a great rock, rent from the sides of Mount Zion by some great national catastrophe and projected into the central plain of China, which has stood there, while the centuries rolled by, sublime in its antiquity and solitude."

# APPENDIX

Not very much is left to be said about the Jews in Kaifengfu after the summary of their sad history given in the previous paper. A short history of events in chronological order would perhaps be helpful in following the decline of the Kaifengfu Colony. This is given at the end of the present paper. A few other important facts, not included in the preceding article, are here given, to make the booklet, as much as possible, a complete record.

## JEWISH COMMUNITIES IN CHINA

While this article mentions only Kaifengfu, Ningpo, Hangchow, and Peking as having been settled by Jewish immigrants, there is reliable evidence to show that several other towns in China have had colonies of Jewish people. Semmedo, a Roman Catholic missionary, who is stated to have mentioned four towns as having Jewish inhabitants, may have had Nanking in mind, in addition to the first three above mentioned, for he visited that town about the middle of the 17th century, and remarked, in his account, that the Jewish colony there was in process of breaking up through lack of teachers, four families having already gone over to the Mahommedan creed. Dr. Fryer, speaking on Chinese Jews in 1902, told his audience of a Chinese official who had mentioned to him that he personally knew some descendants of the colony in Nanking. They were generally well-to-do, the man said, some of them being officials of middle rank, while others were engaged in banking, commerce, etc. The remnants of this colony do not now form part of a Jewish community, and the writer, who has been in Nanking twice recently, found no hint of their existence. A Canadian lady, a resident there for twelve years, and well versed in the history of Nanking and things Chinese in general, has told me that she has never come across any mention of Nanking Jews. She has, however, heard of the Kaifengfu colony, and once met a native peddler of silks who caught her attention by his pronounced un-Chinese and somewhat Jewish appearance. "I know where you come from," she said to him, pointedly. "You come from Kaifengfu." The man admitted that he did.

Yet other towns are known to have contained Jews, in large enough numbers to be noted. That this must be so is evident from the fact that, in the early records, the Jewish population in China is estimated at several thousands of souls. Hangchow was reported by Ricci as having a large community and possessing its own temple. A synagogue also existed at Chinkiang, and a large colony must have existed in Canton, where at one time the Jews, together with Mahommedans and Christians, suffered a terrible massacre.

The largest settlement of Jews must have been in Chang-an (now called Sianfu, in Shensi), the capital of the Empire during the Tang Dynasty. An appreciation of the size of the colony is obtained from the fact that it had as many as four synagogues at one time, a fifth being built during the reign of Cheng-kwan, 630 A.D. At this time, when China was at the height of its civilization, the Jews were large in numbers, and apparently ranked high in political and social status. In fact, it is recorded that an empress dowager of the Wei Dynasty went so far as to abolish all the other religions of China, recognizing only the one of the "Tien Spirit", or the "Spirit of Heaven". Now, "Spirit of Heaven" was the name by which the God of the Jews was known, and Dr. Fryer, who mentions the fact cited, is of the opinion that this religion of the Tien Spirit was none other than the religion of the Jews.

More recently, in 1899, a colony of about five hundred Jews was discovered in Tangchwang, a hundred miles south-west of Kaifengfu, by Col. Lehmann, of the German army then stationed at Tsingtao. He reported that the men were engaged generally in the silk trade, and were, on the whole, well-to-do.

## RECORDS

Not much in the shape of records is now left to us. When the two native envoys were sent in 1851 to Kaifengfu by the Society for the Promotion of Christianity among the Jews, they brought away with them, not only six scrolls of the Law (for which they are said to have paid Tls. 400, about Gold $300), but forty smaller MSS. as well. One of the scrolls was for a time in the museum at Hongkong, and about fifteen years ago was presented by the city authorities to

Ohel Leah Synagogue, who now have it. It is a complete scroll of the Law, in a fine state of preservation, and is eventually destined, so the Synagogue has decided, for the Hebrew University at Jerusalem.

Another is, or was, in the hands of the previously mentioned Society in London.

A PORTION OF "NUMBERS," IN THE TSINANFU INSTITUTE.

Some of the records obtained by this Society are now in the possession of the Hebrew Union College, at Cincinnati.

When the writer was in Tsinanfu, some months ago, he ran across a MS. in the Tsinanfu Institute, of which a photograph is here given. It is a portion of Numbers, from XXII. 2 to XXIII. 13, about twenty pages of a foreign-looking paper, measuring 6 in. x 7 in., and bound in the usual foreign way. The characters are badly formed, and the ink slightly faded. The MS. was presented to the Institute by the Rev. W. W. Lawton, with whom the writer got into touch through a mutual friend.

"The copy of the Jewish scripture that I presented to the Tsinanfu Institute," Mr. Lawton writes in reply, "was secured some fifteen years ago through an old Mahommedan in Kaifeng named Yang. It was when we were first buying land in Kaifeng and this old Mr. Yang was one of the middle-men. He had friends among the Jews in Kaifeng and he and I began talking about them. I got him to see if he could not get me any relics, and these scriptures are what he got. I secured one copy from him as late as three months ago.

In all I have secured six different portions through this same old man. At one time the old man thought the business such a good one, that, as his supply of Jewish scriptures was giving out, he tried to work a little trick on me. He got one page of the scripture carved in wood for printing purposes; then he printed enough of this one page to make ten or twelve small books the size of the one photographed. He had every other page turned upside down for variety. These books he brought to me as ancient relics."

In the Royal Asiatic Society's library at Shanghai one can see a facsimile of some Hebrew MSS. Exodus, Chapt. 1 to 6, and 38 to 40, is mentioned. As to inscriptions found in the Synagogue and elsewhere, a detailed reproduction, with translations in French, is given in Father Tobar's article on the Kaifengfu Jews, in "Varietés Sinologiques No. 17", a paper of very great interest and well worth reading by any body interested.

For a history of the colony, perhaps the most important records left to us now are the stone stèles, inscribed in Chinese, which have already been mentioned in the preceding paper. Four of these stèles are mentioned in the early records of the missionaries; whether this means four different tables of stone, or merely four inscriptions, the writer is not certain: one of the stèles he found in Kaifengfu is inscribed on both sides. This point is raised because, if four different tables are meant, then one of them is definitely lost to us, even in the form of a reproduction of the inscription, or a translation of it. Father Tobar's article—the most com-

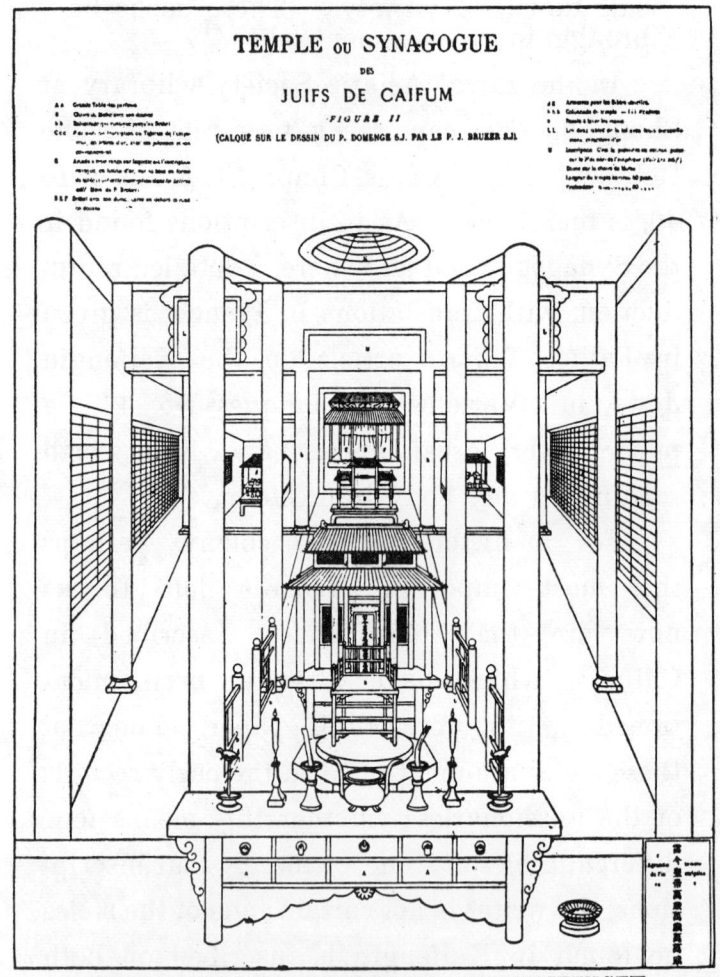

AN 18TH CENTURY SKETCH OF THE KAIFENGFU SYNAGOGUE
(From "Varietés Sinologiques").

plete work on the subject—gives the text of only three tables. As has been mentioned, one of these is inscribed on both sides, making four inscriptions in all. It is more than likely, however, that a fourth table once existed, but no intimation of the date of its inscription or its text is left to us. The four inscriptions of which we have record as regards text are as follows:

1. { Inscribed in 2nd year of the emperor Hung-chih ( 1489)
   Inscribed in 7th year of Cheng-teh ( *circ.* 1512)
2. Inscribed in 2nd year of K'ang-hsi ( *circ.* 1663)
3. Inscribed in 18th year of K'ang-hsi ( *circ.* 1679)

Of these tables, I have seen only the first and the third, both of which are in the custody of the Canadian Church Mission, and are to be found on both sides of the entrance to the mission church on North-South Street (Kaifengfu.) They are huge blocks of stone, roughly 5 ft. by 4 ft. by 6 in., inscribed in characters about an inch high. One of them is inscribed, as is seen above, on both sides; the other only on one side, and is, except for a few stray characters here and there, undecipherable. The first table, with its two inscriptions, is still in a good state of preservation, and rubbings can still be made of it, and the text deciphered. Of the second table, only the heading, in large characters, is legible, and reads, "A stone memorial of the Synagogue," as it was given to me.

On the first table, a few of the family names on the 1489 side are chipped away. The members of the colony say that, during the Boxer uprising, some of their number chipped their names away in order that they might not be identified as foreigners. This fact would tend to show that as recently as 1900, in spite of their apparent merging into the native population, they still considered themselves as of foreign descent. (When, in Kaifengfu, I was introduced to a Mr. Chao, a Chinese Jew who keeps a teashop near the site of the synagogue, he jocularly remarked, in Chinese: "Hah! A member of the same tribe?"—as if to say, *"Och a Yid?"*)

The location of the table of 1663 (which Mr. Ezra gives erroneously as 1668) I have been unable to trace. Some of the early writers on the Kaifengfu Colony give a translation of this inscription, but that is all. The stèle was inscribed by a Chinese mandarin, of Jewish

MR. CHAO AND HIS SON

extraction it is to be presumed, who afterwards became Minister of State. It records the destruction of the temple and the loss of the Scriptures during the 15th year of the Emperor Ts'ung-cheng, of the Ming Dynasty —that is, 1642 A.D., the year the Dynasty was overthrown. At this time, we learn, Kaifengfu was besieged for six months by the rebel forces, and (probably for the same reason that induced the Russians to set fire to Moscow during Napoleon's ill-fated campaign,) the imperial forces within the city flooded it by destroying the Yellow River dykes. The Jewish Settlement was a few hundred yards from the banks of the river, and, as in previous floods, it suffered heavily. Many lost their lives, only some two hundred families escaping. With the destruction of the synagogue, 26 sacred volumes were lost, and from what was rescued, only one Torah could be made out complete.

Ten years later a Jewish Mandarin named Tsao-ying-tseng rebuilt the town, and brought the Jews together again in the vicinity of the synagogue, which he rebuilt in 1653. Whether or not it was the same mandarin who, ten years after that, put up the stone monument I do not know, but it is, of course, most likely.

Such is the story that the stèles tell us, a sad enough story when we think of the spiritual solidarity, the affluence, the social status, that the Jews in China had once enjoyed. No wonder Dr. Martin, though a Christian, was moved to express himself in the following terms, when he came upon one of the tables mentioned:—

> "It is affecting to think of this solitary stone continuing to bear its silent testimony after the synagogue has fallen, and the voice of its worshippers has ceased to be heard. Like that which records the history of the Nestorian Mission in China, it deserves to be regarded as one of the most precious monuments of religious history."

That more information is not left to us is a pity, but it is a mark of the spiritual degeneration into which the community has fallen that they did not hold on zealously to what fire, flood, and insurrection had not taken from them. Speaking of some rubbings taken from some tablets, Father Tobar, somewhat mockingly, says:—

> "Si quelque voyageur Européen passant par Kaifong voulait voir les steles en question, it sera content de savoir qu'au commencement de 1898 l'une d'elles se

SOME OF THE WOMEN & CHILDREN OF THE KAIFENGFU COLONY. (1912)

trouvait dans une cuisine, et l'autre près des latrines, à l'intérieur de la maison d'un des Juifs de la ville."

## THE RESCUE OF THE CHINESE JEWS

During the past three-quarters of a century there have been various attempts to bring spiritual and material help to the stricken colony. About the middle of the last century, attempts in that direction were made both in England and in America. In England, the leader of the proposed expedition died; in America, the Civil War came and put a stop to all proceedings.

James Finn, who at one time held a diplomatic post at Jerusalem, interested himself in the Kaifengfu Jews. In "The Orphan Colony of Jews in China," written by him in 1872, he gives the text of a letter which had been drawn up in Hebrew and Chinese, about 1840, and which, through the kind offices of the British Consul at Amoy, reached Kaifengfu. The reply to this was not received till thirty years later, and was truly pathetic in its contents. "Daily, with tears in our eyes," it read, "we call on the Holy Name. If we could but again procure ministers and put our house of prayer in order, our religion would have a firm support." Poor, suffering, brothers of ours! With what heartaches their elders must have viewed the condition into which the community was rapidly falling.

Somewhat after the middle of the last century, Bishop Schereschewsky, a Jew by birth, induced twelve of the more promising youths of the colony to come to Peking, where he tried to give them a liberal education, including the study of Hebrew. Unfortunately, the life away from home did not satisfy them, and one by one they travelled back.

An appeal similar to that made by Dr. Martin in the New York "Jewish Times," was voiced by Dr. Fryer when speaking in 1902 before the Council of Jewish Women, in San Francisco. He gave practical suggestions for relief and urged some young man or woman to go out as a missionary, study the language and the people, and thus win them back to Judaism. Judaism, however, was not, and is not today, ready for such sacrifices. A non-prosletyzing religion, upholding the right of each man to travel God's path in his own way, it has yet lived to reach the anomalous position of being powerless to render assistance to its own estranged sons and daughters! Would that we were a little more militant and aggressive, not in combating the religion of others, but at least in safeguarding our own. The swallowing-up of Jewish communities such as those in China would not then have been possible.

On March 13th, 1900, a letter in Hebrew and Chinese was sent by messengers from the Jewish Community at Shanghai, to that in Kaifengfu, which deserves recording here. Part of it read as follows:—

> "We assure you that we are eager to help you according to our ability, so that you may walk again in the footsteps of your forefathers. If you desire to rebuild the House of God, which is now become a waste place, we will collect money and send it to you; if you want a teacher to instruct you, we will send you one; if it should please you to come hither and settle here in the city of Shanghai, we will help you to do so, and put you in the way to earn a livelihood by starting you in trade, and all that you may require we will endeavour to supply you with, for there are in this city men of our faith, great and wealthy, men of affairs and business, who can help to maintain yourselves and your sons and daughters.

> "Wherefore we beg you not to part with scrolls still left to you. On this letter reaching you, send two or three men to us whom we may question, and from whom we can find out what we can do for you.

We will pay all the expenses of the messengers; we will give them their sustenance, and pay them their expenses until they reach again your city.''

The results of this communication are already recorded in the preceding paper. At that time the Society for the Rescue of the Chinese Jews was first formed, and in its Minutes we read of the difficulties that faced this new attempt to bring succour to the fast dying community. The Boxer Rebellion had broken out, and naturally, communications were interefered with. One entry speaks of a letter which Mr. Powell, of the China Inland Mission, kindly consented to carry to the colony. In a riot that occurred on the way, the letter, among other valuables, was lost, Mr. Powell narrowly escaping with his life.

In 1903 Mr. Shekury offered to go on a mission of investigation, and next year General Mesney signified his willingness to do likewise. No further entries are recorded in the Minutes-book, and we are left to infer that nothing more was done.

Recently, interest has been again revived in the fate of this Orphan Colony, and it was thought expedient to reorganize the Society for the Rescue of the Chinese Jews. This was accordingly done, and at an illustrated lecture before the Jewish community here I had the opportunity of describing my recent findings in Kaifengfu, and to recount the history of the colony, in which Mr. Geo. E. Sokolsky collaborated in describing the route along which the Jews travelled across Asia to China. The result of the meeting was that a representative of the Society, Mr. Wong (David Levy), a Sinkiang (Chinese Turkestan) Jew, was sent some time ago to Kaifengfu to get more intimate details than could be obtained by a foreigner. A few weeks ago, he sent us the following:—

> "On the 13th of August we took a picture in the garden of the American Church Mission [in whose compound the tablets before mentioned are to be found] at which more than ten people were present, all of them heads of families [descended from Jewish stock]. The next morning at ten I gave a talk at the Mission, attended by about a thousand people, Jews and Christians. After the meeting I asked two Jews, Mr. Chao and Mr. Shih Chung-yung, to make a plan of the synagogue property and to write the enclosed report."

The report enclosed with the letter stated that so far as investigatious showed, there were but 99 Jews left in Kaifengfu, most of them very poor, only a few families being well-to-do. The plan of the synagogue represents a plot of ground about 480ft. by 240ft., within which are some private dwellings and other build-

THE SITE OF THE KAIFENGFU SYNAGOGUE

ings, the names of whose owners are mentioned. One of the houses, which Mr. Zao owns, he is willing to contribute towards the plan of helping the Jews of the town. The report

MR. WONG (DAVID LEVY)

furthermore gives a list of names of the Kaifengfu Jews, men, women, and children, their ages, occupations, etc., which will prove useful in getting them together again into a

GROUP OF LEADING JEWS OF KAIFENGFU. (MR. WONG STANDS AT THE RIGHT. A FRIENDLY CHINESE-CHRISTIAN PASTOR STANDS AT THE LEFT.)

community. It ends up with the statement that the two gentlemen above-mentioned are continuing their investigations and that we will hear from them again.

"JEWISH COLONY" LANE

Since the receipt of the above letter, Mr. Wong has had time to return to Shanghai and make his report in person. What he has had to say has been indeed encouraging and has done much to raise the hope that once again Kaifengfu might become the center of a Jewish Colony, as true to its memories and traditions as it originally was. Mr. Wong has gone into the homes of those he believed to be descended of Jewish stock and has spoken to them, getting their views regarding the problem of reorganizing the Jewish Colony. They seem to be interested in the project, he says, and have suggested that a school be built first, and the younger generation instructed in the rudiments of Jewish faith. Towards this end, as soon as sufficient money has been collected, Mr. Wong has expressed his willingness to move his family to Kaifengfu and take up his abode there, devoting the remaining years of his life to the instruction of these people. One hopeful element stands out from the otherwise disorganized condition of the colony: though they have not for many, many a year met as a congregation or community, they yet recognize a communal leader, Mr. Chao Yuen Chung by name, and the fact that they still regard themselves as of Jewish parentage, encourages one to think that the prospect of communal reorganization is not such a hopeless one after all.

Unfortunately, the deed to the site of the synagogue has now passed out of the hands of the Jewish community at Kaifengfu, and is in that of the Canadian Church Mission, who bought the land. A little street leading off from this site is still known by the name of "Jewish Colony Lane," and two brick arches found over that lane proclaim the fact. The surrounding houses, or rather, huts, could be purchased as a center for communal life, and the scattered descendants of the Colony brought together again around a site hallowed by the memory of a common bond. The two stone stèles, now in the custody of the Mission, would then revert to the Colony. From one of the leaders of the community, the Mission also purchased a stone laver, which had once formed part of the synagogue property. This no doubt could also be re-purchased and given back to the newly organized colony, along with what Scriptures and Manuscripts could be brought together to give them a touch of their glorious past.

THE LAVER, ONCE PART OF THE SYNAGOGUE PROPERTY.

The difficulties that faced would-be rescuers in previous years no longer face us now. At that time, travel was both difficult and dangerous. Now it is no longer so. The 470 miles that Dr. Martin records having traversed in a month, from Peking to Kaifengfu, can now be covered by train in a few hours.

Thus the situation now stands. The outlook is more hopeful than it ever has been since the idea of rescue work first took hold. The miracle, if not again delayed, may yet be accomplished and these sons of Abraham and of Moses rescued from the very jaws of total annihilation.

| | | |
|---|---|---|
| *(circ.)* | 1836 | Last Rabbi dies; disorganization begins |
| | 1849 | Disastrous flood sweeps away Synagogue; large losses in Jewish lives |
| | 1851 | Two Chinese sent by Christian Mission report Synagogue in dilapidated condition. Bought scrolls of the Law and many manuscripts, which they carried away. |
| *(circ.)* | „ | Expeditions of relief are attempted in England and America, with no success<br>Bishop Schereshewsky brings twelve of the colony to Peking for instruction |
| | 1860 | Massacre and flood in Kaifengfu; Taiping Rebellion. Up to this time, it is noted, no intermarriages have taken place |
| | 1866 | Rev. Martin visits colony and finds no circumcision, no rites, no festivals observed. Synagogue demolished by colonists |
| | 1900 | "Society for the Rescue of the Chinese Jews" organized in Shanghai. Some colonists brought down and instructed |
| | 1902 | Two colonists come to Shanghai; one is circumcized |
| | 1924 | "Society for the Rescue of the Chinese Jews" revived, and a Chinese Jew sent to make investigations. Finds but 99 souls left showing Jewish descent |